The American Mind

By
Bliss Perry

THE AMERICAN MIND

I

Race, Nation, and Book

Many years ago, as a student in a foreign university, I remember attacking, with the complacency of youth, a German history of the English drama, in six volumes. I lost courage long before the author reached the age of Elizabeth, but I still recall the subject of the opening chapter: it was devoted to the physical geography of Great Britain. Writing, as the good German professor did, in the triumphant hour of Taine's theory as to the significance of place, period, and environment in determining the character of any literary production, what could be more logical than to begin at the beginning? Have not the chalk cliffs guarding the southern coast of England, have not the fatness of the midland counties and the soft rainy climate of a North Atlantic island, and the proud, tenacious, self-assertive folk that are bred there, all left their trace upon A Midsummer Night's Dream, and Every Man in his Humour and She Stoops to Conquer? Undoubtedly. Latitude and longitude, soil and rainfall and food-supply, racial origins and crossings, political and social and economic conditions, must assuredly leave their marks upon the mental and artistic productiveness of a people and upon the personality of individual writers.

Taine, who delighted to point out all this, and whose English Literature remains a monument of the defects as well as of the advantages of his method, was of course not the inventor of the climatic theory. It is older than Aristotle, who discusses it in his treatise on Politics. It was a topic of interest to the scholars of the Renaissance. Englishmen of the seventeenth century, with an unction of pseudo-science added to their natural patriotism, discovered in the English climate one of the reasons of England's greatness. Thomas Sprat, writing in 1667 on the History of the Royal Society, waxes bold and asserts: "If there can be a true character given of the Universal Temper of any Nation under Heaven, then certainly this must be ascribed to our countrymen, that they have commonly an unaffected sincerity, that they love to deliver their minds with a sound simplicity, that they have the middle qualities between the reserved, subtle southern and the rough, unhewn northern people, that they are not extremely prone to speak, that they are more concerned what others will think of the strength than of the fineness of what they say, and that a universal modesty possesses them. These qualities are so conspicuous and proper to the soil that we often hear them objected to us by some of our neighbor Satyrists in more disgraceful expressions.... Even the position of our climate, the air, the influence of the heaven, the composition of the English blood, as well as the embraces of the Ocean, seem to join with the labours of the Royal Society to render our country a Land of Experimental Knowledge."

The excellent Sprat was the friend and executor of the poet Cowley, who has in the Preface to his Poems a charming passage about the relation of literature to the external circumstances in which it is written.

"If wit be such a Plant that it scarce receives heat enough to keep it alive even in the summer of our cold Clymate, how can it choose but wither in a long and a sharp winter? a warlike, various and a tragical age is best to write of, but worst to write in." And he adds this, concerning his own art of poetry: "There is nothing that requires so much serenity and chearfulness of spirit; it must not be either overwhelmed with the cares of Life, or overcast with the Clouds of Melancholy and Sorrow, or shaken and disturbed with the storms of injurious Fortune; it must, like the Halcyon, have fair weather to breed in. The Soul must be filled with bright and delightful Idaeas, when it undertakes to communicate delight to others, which is the main end of Poesie. One may see through the stile of Ovid de Trist., the humbled and dejected condition of Spirit with which he wrote it; there scarce remains any footstep of that Genius, Quem nec Jovis ira, nec ignes, etc. The cold of the country has strucken through all his faculties, and benummed the very feet of his Verses."

Madame de Staël's Germany, one of the most famous of the "national character" books, begins with a description of the German landscape. But though nobody, from Ovid in exile down to Madame de Staël, questions the general significance of place, time, and circumstances as affecting the nature of a literary product, when we come to the exact and as it were mathematical demonstration of the precise workings of these physical influences, our generation is distinctly more cautious than were the literary critics of forty years ago. Indeed, it is a hundred years since Fisher Ames, ridiculing the theory that climate acts directly upon literary products, said wittily of Greece: "The figs are as fine as ever, but where are the Pindars?" The theory of race, in particular, has been sharply questioned by the experts. "Saxon" and "Norman," for example, no longer seem to us such simple terms as sufficed for the purpose of Scott's Ivanhoe or of Thierry's Norman Conquest, a book inspired by Scott's romance. The late Professor Freeman, with characteristic bluntness, remarked of the latter book: "Thierry says at the end of his work that there are no longer either Normans or Saxons except in history.... But in Thierry's sense of the word, it would be truer to say that there never were 'Normans' or 'Saxons' anywhere, save in the pages of romances like his own."

There is a brutal directness about this verdict upon a rival historian which we shall probably persist in calling "Saxon"; but it is noworse than the criticisms of Matthew Arnold's essay on "The Celtic Spirit" made to-day by university professors who happen to know Old Irish at first hand, and consequently consider Arnold's opinion on Celtic matters to be hopelessly amateurish.

The wiser scepticism of our day concerning all hard-and-fast racial distinctions has been admirably summed up by Josiah Royce. "A race psychology," he declares, "is still a science for the future to discover.... We do not scientifically know what the true racial varieties of mental type really are. No doubt there are such varieties. The judgment day, or the science of the future, may demonstrate what they are. We are at present very ignorant regarding the whole matter."

Nowhere have the extravagances of the application of racial theories to intellectual products been more pronounced than in the fields of art and literature. Audiences listen to a waltz which the programme declares to be an adaptation of a Hungarian folk-song, and though they may be more ignorant of Hungary than Shakespeare was of Bohemia, they have no hesitation in exclaiming: "How truly Hungarian this is!" Or, it may be, how truly "Japanese" is this vase which was made in Japan—perhaps for the American market; or how intensely "Russian" is this melancholy tale by Turgenieff. This prompt deduction of racial qualities from works of art which themselves give the critic all the information he possesses about the races in question,—or, in other words, the enthusiastic assertion that a thing is like itself,—is one of the familiar notes of amateur criticism. It is travelling in a circle, and the corregiosity of Corregio is the next station.

Blood tells, no doubt, and a masterpiece usually betrays some token of the place and hour of its birth. A knowledge of the condition of political parties in Athens in 416 B.C. adds immensely to the enjoyment of the readers of Aristophanes; the fun becomes funnier and the daring even more splendid than before. Molière's training as an actor does affect the dramaturgic quality of his comedies. All this is demonstrable, and to the prevalent consciousness of it our generation is deeply indebted to Taine and his pupils. But before displaying dogmatically the inevitable brandings of racial and national traits on a national literature, before pointing to this and that unmistakable evidence of local or temporal influence on the form or spirit of a masterpiece, we are now inclined to make some distinct reservations. These reservations are not without bearing upon our own literature in America.

There are, for instance, certain artists who seem to escape the influences of the time-spirit. The most familiar example is that of Keats. He can no doubt be assigned to the George the Fourth period by a critical examination of his vocabulary, but the characteristic political and social movements of that epoch in England left him almost untouched. Edgar Allan Poe might have written some of his tales in the seventeenth century or in the twentieth; he might, like Robert Louis Stevenson, have written in Samoa rather than in the Baltimore, Philadelphia, or New York of his day; his description of the Ragged Mountains of Virginia, within very sight of the university which he attended, was borrowed, in the good old convenient fashion, from Macaulay; in fact, it requires something of Poe's own ingenuity to find in Poe, who is one of the indubitable assets of American literature, anything distinctly American.

Wholly aside from such spiritual insulation of the single writer, there is the obvious fact that none of the arts, not even literature, and not all of them together, can furnish a wholly adequate representation of racial or national characteristics. It is well known to-day that the so-called "classic" examples of Greek art, most of which were brought to light and discoursed upon by critics from two to four centuries ago, represent but a single phase of Greek feeling; and that the Greeks, even in what we choose to call their most characteristic period, had a distinctly "romantic" tendency which their more recently discovered plastic art betrays. But even if we had all the lost statues, plays, poems, and orations, all the Greek paintings about which we know so little, and the Greek music about which we know still less, does anybody suppose that this wealth of artistic expression would furnish a wholly satisfactory notion of the racial and psychological traits of the Greek people?

One may go even further. Does a truly national art exist anywhere, — an art, that is to say, which conveys a trustworthy and adequate expression of the national temper as a whole? We have but to reflect upon the European and American judgments, during the last thirtyyears, concerning the representative quality of the art of Japan, and to observe how many of those facile generalizations about the Japanese character, deduced from vases and prints and enamel, were smashed to pieces by the Russo-Japanese War. This may illustrate the blunders of foreign criticism, perhaps, rather than any inadequacy in the racially representative character of Japanese art. But it is impossible that critics, and artists themselves, should not err, in the conscious endeavor to pronounce upon the infinitely complex materials with which they are called upon to deal. We must confess that the expression of racial and national characteristics, by means of only one art, such as literature, or by all the arts together, is at best imperfect, and is always likely to be misleading unless corroborated by other evidence.

For it is to be remembered that in literature, as in the other fields of artistic activity, we are dealing with the question of form; of securing a concrete and pleasurable embodiment of certain emotions. It may well happen that literature not merely fails to give an adequate report of the racial or national or personal emotions felt during a given epoch, but that it fails to report these emotions at all. Not only the "old, unhappy, far-off" things of racial experience, but the new and delight-giving experiences of the hour, may lack their poet. Widespread moods of public elation or wistfulness or depression have passed without leaving a shadow upon the mirror of art. There was no one to hold the mirror or even to fashion it. No note of Renaissance criticism, whether in Italy, France, or England, is more striking, and in a way more touching, than the universal feeling that in the rediscovery of the classics men had found at last the "terms of art," the rules and methods of a game which they had long wished to be playing. Englishmen and Frenchmen of the sixteenth century will not allow that their powers are less virile, their emotions less eager, than those of the Greeks and Romans. Only, lacking the very terms of art, they had not been able to arrive at fit expression; the soul had found no body wherewith to clothe itself into beauty. As they avowed in all simplicity, they needed schoolmasters; the discipline of Aristotle and Horace and Virgil; a body of critical doctrine, to teach them how to express the France and England or Italy of their day, and thus give permanence to their fleeting vision of the world. Naïve as may have been the Renaissance expression of this need of formal training, blind as it frequently was to the beauty which we recognize in the undisciplined vernacular literatures of mediæval Europe, those groping scholars were essentially right. No one can paint or compose by nature. One must slowly master an art of expression.

Now through long periods of time, and over many vast stretches of territory, as our own American writing abundantly witnesses, the whole formal side of expression may be neglected. "Literature," in its narrower sense, may not exist. In that restricted and higher meaning of the term, literature has always been uncommon enough, even in Athens or Florence. It demands not merely personal distinction or power, not merely some uncommon height or depth or breadth of capacity and insight, but a purely artistic training, which in the very nature of the case is rare. Millions of Russians, perhaps, have felt about the general problems of life much as Turgenieff felt, but they lacked the sheer literary art with which the Notes of a Sportsman was written. Thousands of frontier lawyers and politicians shared Lincoln's hard and varied and admirable training in the mastery of speech, but in his hands alone was the weapon wrought to such perfection of temper and weight and edge that he spoke and wrote literature without knowing it.

Such considerations belong, I am aware, to the accepted commonplaces, — perhaps to what William James used to call "the unprofitable delineation of the obvious." Everybody recognizes that literary gifts imply an exceptionally rich development of general human capacities, together with a professional aptitude and training of which but few men are capable. There is but one lumberman in camp who can play the fiddle, though the whole camp can dance. Thus the great book, we are forever saying, is truly representative of myriads of minds in a certain degree of culture, although but one man could have written it. The writing member of a family is often the one who acquires notoriety and a bank account, but he is likely to have candid friends who admit, though not always in his presence, that, aside from this one professional gift and practice, he is not intellectually or emotionally or spiritually superior to his brothers and sisters. Waldo Emerson thought himself the intellectual inferior of his brother Charles; and good observers loved to maintain that John Holmes was wittier than Oliver Wendell, and Ezekiel Webster a better lawyer than Daniel.

Applied to the literary history of a race, this principle is suggestive. We must be slow to affirm that, because certain ideas and feelings did not attain, in this or that age or place, to purely literary expression, they were therefore not in existence. The men and women of the colonial period in our own country, for instance, have been pretty uniformly declared to have been deficient in the sense of beauty. What is the evidence? It is mostly negative. They produced no poetry, fiction, painting, sculpture, or music worthy of the name. They were predominantly Puritan, and the whole world has been informed that English Puritanism was hostile to Art. They were preoccupied with material and moral concerns. Even if they had remained in England, Professor Trent affirms, these contemporaries of Milton and Bunyan would have produced no art or literature. Now it is quite true that for nearly two hundred years after the date of the first settlement of the American colonists, opportunities for cultivating the arts did not exist. But that the sense of beauty was wholly atrophied, I, for one, do not believe. The passionate eagerness with which the forefathers absorbed the noblest of all poetry and prose in the pages of their one book, the Bible; the unwearied curiosity and care with which those farmers and fishermen and woodsmen read the signs of the sky; their awe of the dark wilderness and their familiar traffic with the great deep; the silences of lonely places; the opulence of primeval meadows by the clear streams; the English flowers that were made to bloom again in farmhouse windows and along garden walks; the inner visions, more lovely still, of duty and of moral law; the spirit of sacrifice; the daily walk with God, whether by green pastures of the spirit or through ways that were dark and terrible; — is there in all this no discipline of the soul in moral beauty, and no training of the eye to perceive the exquisite harmonies of the visible earth? It is true that the Puritans had no professional men of letters; it is true that doctrinal sermons provided their chief intellectual sustenance; true that their lives were stern, and that many of the softer emotions were repressed. But beauty may still be traced in the fragments of their recorded speech, in their diaries and letters and phrases of devotion. You will search the eighteenth century of old England in vain for such ecstasies of wonder at the glorious beauty of the universe as were penned by Jonathan Edwards in his youthful Diary. There is every presumption, from what we know of the two men, that Whittier's father and grandfather were peculiarly sensitive to the emotions of home and neighborhood and domesticity which their gifted descendant—too physically frail to be absorbed in the rude labor of the farm—has embodied in Snow-Bound. The Quaker poet knew that he surpassed his forefathers in facility in verse-making, but he would have been amused (as his Margaret Smith's Journal proves) at the notion that his ancestors were without a sense of beauty or that they lacked responsiveness to the chords of fireside sentiment. He was simply the only Whittier, except his sister Elizabeth, who had ever found leisure, as old-fashioned correspondents used to say, "to take his pen in hand." This leisure developed in him the sense—latent no doubt in his ancestors—of the beauty of words, and the excitement of rhythm. Emerson's Journal in the eighteen-thirties glows with a Dionysiac rapture over what he calls "delicious days"; but did the seven generations of clergymen from whom Emerson descended have no delicious and haughty and tender days that passed unrecorded? Formal literature perpetuates and glorifies many aspects of individual and national experience; but how much eludes it wholly, or is told, if at all, in broken syllables, in Pentecostal tongues that seem to be our own and yet are unutterably strange!

To confess thus that literature, in the proper sense of the word, represents but a narrow segment of personal or racial experience, is very far from a denial of the genuineness and the significance of the affirmations which literature makes. We recognize instinctively that Whittier's Snow-Bound is a truthful report, not merely of a certain farmhouse kitchen in East Haverhill, Massachusetts, during the early nineteenth century, but of a mode of thinking and feeling which is widely diffused wherever the Anglo-Saxon race has wandered. Perhaps Snow-Bound lacks a certain universality of suggestiveness which belongs to a still more famous poem, The Cotter's Saturday Night of Burns, but both of these portrayals of rustic simplicity and peace owe their celebrity to their truly representative character. They are evidence furnished by a single art, as to a certain mode and coloring of human existence; but every corroboration of that evidence heightens our admiration for the artistic sincerity and insight of the poet. To draw an illustration from a more splendid epoch, let us remind ourselves that the literature of the "spacious times of great Elizabeth"—a period of strong national excitement, and one deeply representative of the very noblest and most permanent traits of English national character—was produced within startlingly few years and in a local territory extremely limited. The very language in which that literature is clothed was spoken only by the court, by a couple of counties, and at the two universities. Its prose and verse were frankly experimental. It is true that such was the emotional ferment of the score of years preceding the Armada, that great captains and voyagers who scarcely wrote a line were hailed as kings of the realm of imagination, and that Puttenham, in phrases which that generation could not have found extravagant, inscribes his book on Poetry to Queen Elizabeth as the "most excellent Poet" of the age. Well, the glorified political images may grow dim or tawdry with time, but the poetry has endured, and it is everywhere felt to be a truly national, a deeply racial product. Its time and place and hour were all local; but the Canadian and the American, the South African and Australasian Englishman feels that that Elizabethan poetry is his poetry still.

When we pass, therefore, as we must shortly do, to the consideration of this and that literary product of America, and to the scrutiny of the really representative character of our books, we must bear in mind that the questions concerning the race, the place, the hour, the man,—questions so familiar to modern criticism,—remain valid and indeed essential; but that in applying them to American writing there are certain allowances, qualifications, adjustments of the scale of values, which are no less important to an intelligent perception of the quality of our literature. This task is less simple than the critical assessment of a typical German or French or Scandinavian writer, where the strain of blood is unmixed, the continuity of literary tradition unbroken, the precise impact of historical and personal influences more easy to estimate. I open, for example, any one of half a dozen French studies of Balzac. Here is a many-sided man, a multifarious writer, a personality that makes ridiculous the merely formal pigeon-holing and labelling processes of professional criticism. And yet with what perfect precision of method and certainty of touch do Le Breton, for example, or Brunetière, in their books on Balzac, proceed to indicate those impulses of race and period and environment which affected the character of Balzac's novels! The fact that he was born in Tours in 1799 results in the inevitable and inevitably expert paragraphs about Gallic blood, and the physical exuberance of the Touraine surroundings of his youth, and the post-revolutionary tendency to disillusion and analysis. And so with Balzac's education, his removal to Paris in the Restoration period, his ventures in business and his affairs of love, his admiration for Shakespeare and for Fenimore Cooper; his mingled Romanticism and Realism; his Titanism and his childishness; his stupendous outline for the Human Comedy; and his scarcely less astounding actual achievement. All this is discussed by his biographers with the professional dexterity of critics trained intellectually in the Latin traditions and instinctively aware of the claims of race, biographers familiar with every page of French history, and profoundly interested, like their readers, in every aspect of French life. Alas, we may say, in despairing admiration of such workmanship, "they order these things better in France." And they do; but racial unity, and long lines of national literary tradition, make these things easier to order than they are with us. The intellectual distinction of American critical biographies like Lounsbury's Cooper or Woodberry's Hawthorne is all the more notable because we possess such a slender body of truly critical doctrine native to our own soil; because our national literary tradition as to available material and methods is hardly formed; because the very word "American" has a less precise connotation than the word "New Zealander."

Let us suppose, for instance, that like Professor Woodberry a few years ago, we were asked to furnish a critical study of Hawthorne. The author of The Scarlet Letter is one of the most justly famous of American writers. But precisely what national traits are to be discovered in this eminent fellow-countryman of ours? We turn, like loyal disciples of Taine and Sainte-Beuve, to his ancestral stock. We find that it is English as far back as it can be traced; as purely English as the ancestry of Dickens or Thackeray, and more purely English than the ancestry of Browning or Burke or His Majesty George the Fifth. Was Hawthorne, then, simply an Englishman living in America? He himself did not think so, — as his English Note-Books abundantly prove. But just what subtle racial differentiation had been at work, since William Hawthorne migrated to Massachusetts with Winthrop in 1630? Here we face, unless I am mistaken, that troublesome but fascinating question of Physical Geography. Climate, soil, food, occupation, religious or moral preoccupation, social environment, Salem witchcraft and Salem seafaring had all laid their invisible hands upon the physical and intellectual endowment of the child born in 1804. Does this make Nathaniel Hawthorne merely an "Englishman with a difference," as Mr. Kipling, born in India, is an "Englishman with a difference"? Hawthorne would have smiled, or, more probably, he would have sworn, at such a question. He considered himself an American Democrat; in fact a contra mundum

Democrat, for good or for ill. Is it, then, a political theory, first put into full operation in this country a scant generation before Hawthorne's birth, which made him un-English? We must walk warily here. Our Canadian neighbors of English stock have much the same climate, soil, occupations, and preoccupations as the inhabitants of the northern territory of the United States. They have much the same courts, churches, and legislatures. They read the same books and magazines. They even prefer baseball to cricket. They are loyal adherents of a monarchy, but they are precisely as free, as self-governing, and—in the social sense of the word—as "democratic"—in spite of the absence of a republican form of government—as the citizens of that "land of the free and home of the brave" which lies to the south of them. Yet Canadian literature, one may venture to affirm, has remained to this hour a "colonial" literature, or, if one prefers the phrase, a literature of "Greater Britain." Was Hawthorne possibly right in his instinct that politics did make a difference, and that in writing The Marble Faun,—the scene of which is laid in Rome,—or The House of the Seven Gables,—which is a story of Salem,—he was consistently engaged in producing, not "colonial" or "Greater-British" but distinctly American literature? We need not answer this question prematurely, if we wish to reserve our judgment, but it is assuredly one of the questions which the biographers and critics of our men of letters must ultimately face and answer.

Furthermore, the student of literature produced in the United States of America must face other questions almost as complicated as this of race. In fact, when we choose Hawthorne as a typical case in which to observe the American refashioning of the English temper into something not English, we are selecting a very simple problem compared with the complexities which have resulted from the mingling of various European stocks upon American soil. But take, for the moment, the mere obvious matter of expanse of territory. We are obliged to reckon, not with a compact province such as those in which many Old World literatures have been produced, but with what our grandfathers considered a "boundless continent." This vast national domain was long ago "organized" for political purposes: but so far as literature is concerned it remains unorganized to-day. We have, as has been constantly observed, no literary capital, like London or Paris, to serve as the seat of centralized authority; no code of literary procedure and conduct; no "lawgivers of Parnassus"; no supreme court of letters, whose judgments are recognized and obeyed. American public opinion asserts itself with singular unanimity and promptness in the field of politics. In literary matters we remain in the stage of anarchic individualism, liable to be stampeded from time to time by mob-excitement over a popular novel or moralistic tract, and then disintegrating, as before, into an incoherent mass of individually intelligent readers.

The reader who has some personal acquaintance with the variations of type in different sections of this immense territory of ours finds his curiosity constantly stimulated by the presence of sectional and local characteristics. There are sharply cut provincial peculiarities, of course, in Great Britain and in Germany, in Italy and Spain, and in all of the countries a corresponding "regional" literature has been developed. Our provincial variations of accent and vocabulary, in passing from North to South or East to West, are less striking, on the whole, than the dialectical differences found in the various English counties. But our general uniformity of grammar and the comparatively slight variations in spoken accent cover an extraordinary variety of local and sectional modes of thinking and feeling. The reader of American short stories and lyrics must constantly ask himself: Is this truth to local type consistent with the main trend of American production? Is this merely a bit of Virginia or Texas or California, or does it, while remaining no less Southern or Western in its local coloring, suggest also the ampler light, the wide generous air of the United States of America?

The observer of this relationship between local and national types will find some American communities where all the speech or habitual thought is of the future. Foreigners usually consider such communities the most typically "American," as doubtless they are; but there are other sections, still more faithfully exploited by local writers, where the mood is wistful and habitually regards the past. America, too, like the Old World, — and in New England more than elsewhere, — has her note of decadence, of disillusion, of autumnal brightness and transiency. Some sections of the country, and notably the slave-holding states in the forty years preceding the Civil War, have suffered widespread intellectual blight. The best talent of the South, for a generation, went into politics, in the passionately loyal endeavor to prop up a doomed economic and social system; and the loss to the intellectual life of the country cannot be reckoned. Over vast sections of our prosperous and intelligent people of the Mississippi Basin to-day the very genius of commonplaceness seems to hover. Take the great State of Iowa, with its well-to-do and homogeneous population, its fortunate absence of perplexing city-problems, its general air of prosperity and content. It is a typical state of the most typically American portion of the country; but it breeds no books. Yet in Indiana, another state of the same general conditions as to population and prosperity, and only one generation further removed than Iowa from primitive pioneer conditions, books are produced at a rate which provokes a universal American smile. I do not affirm that the literary critic is bound to answer all such local puzzles as this. But he is bound at least to reflect upon them, and to demand of every local literary product throughout this varied expanse of states: Is the root of the "All-American" plant growing here, or is it not?

Furthermore, the critic must pursue this investigation of national traits in our writing, not only over a wide and variegated territory, but through a very considerable sweep of time. American literature is often described as "callow," as the revelation of "national inexperience," and in other similar terms. It is true that we had no professional men of letters before Irving and that the blossoming time of the notable New England group of writers did not come until nearly the middle of the nineteenth century. But we have had time enough, after all, to show what we wish to be and what we are. There have been European books about America ever since the days of Columbus; it is three hundred years since the first books were written in America. Modern English prose, the language of journalism, of science, of social intercourse, came into being only in the early eighteenth century, in the age of Queen Anne. But Cotton Mather'sMagnalia, a vast book dealing with the past history of New England, was printed in 1702, only a year later than Defoe's True-Born Englishman. For more than two centuries the development of English speech and English writing on this side of the Atlantic has kept measurable pace—now slower, now swifter—with the speech of the mother country. When we recall the scanty term of years within which was produced the literature of the age of Elizabeth, it seems like special pleading to insist that America has not yet had time to learn or recite her bookish lessons.

This is not saying that we have had a continuous or adequate development, either of the intellectual life, or of literary expression. There are certain periods of strong intellectual movement, of heightened emotion, alike in the colonial epoch and since the adoption of our present form of government, in which it is natural to search for revelations of those qualities which we now feel to be essential to our national character. Certain epochs of our history, in other words, have been peculiarly "American," and have furnished the most ideal expression of national tendencies.

If asked to select the three periods of our history which in this sense have been most significant, most of us, I imagine, would choose the first vigorous epoch of New England Puritanism, say from 1630 to 1676; then, the epoch of the great Virginians, say from 1766 to 1789; and finally the epoch of distinctly national feeling, in which New England and the West were leaders, between 1830 and 1865. Those three generations have been the most notable in the three hundred years since the permanent settlements began. Each of them has revealed, in a noble fashion, the political, ethical, and emotional traits of our people; and although the first two of the three periods concerned themselves but little with literary expression of the deep-lying characteristics of our stock, the expression is not lacking. Thomas Hooker's sermon on the "Foundation of Political Authority," John Winthrop's grave advice on the "Nature of Liberty," Jefferson's "Declaration," Webster's "Reply to Hayne," Lincoln's "Inaugurals," are all fundamentally American. They are political in their immediate purpose, but, like the speeches of Edmund Burke, they are no less literature because they are concerned with the common needs and the common destiny. Hooker and Winthrop wrote before our formal national existence began; Jefferson, at the hour of the nation's birth; and Lincoln, in the day of its sharpest trial. Yet, though separated from one another by long intervals of time, the representative figures of the three epochs, English in blood and American in feeling, are not so unlike as one might think. A thorough grasp of our literature thus requires—and in scarcely less a degree than the mastery of one of the literatures of Europe—a survey of a long period, the search below the baffling or contradictory surface of national experience for the main drift of that experience, and the selection of the writers, of one generation after another, who have given the most fit and permanent and personalized expression to the underlying forces of the national life.

There is another preliminary word which needs no less to be said. It concerns the question of international influences upon nationalliterature. Our own generation has been taught by many events that no race or country can any longer live "to itself." Internationalism is in the very atmosphere: and not merely as regards politics in the narrowed sense, but with reference to questions of economics, sociology, art, and letters. The period of international isolation of the United States, we are rather too fond of saying, closed with the Spanish-American War. It would be nearer the truth to say that so far as the things of the mind and the spirit are concerned, there has never been any absolute isolation. The Middle West, from the days of Jackson to Lincoln, that raw West described by Dickens and Mrs. Trollope, comes nearer isolation than any other place or time. The period of the most eloquent assertions of American independence in artistic and literary matters was the epoch of New England Transcendentalism, which was itself singularly cosmopolitan in its literary appetites. The letters and journals of Emerson, Whitman, and Thoreau show the strong European meat on which these men fed, just before their robust declarations of our self-sufficiency. But there is no real self-sufficiency, and Emerson and Whitman themselves, in other moods, have written most suggestive passages upon our European inheritances and affiliations.

The fortunes of the early New England colonies, in fact, were followed by Protestant Europe with the keen solicitude and affection of kinsmen. Oliver Cromwell signs his letter to John Cotton in 1651, "Your affectionate friend to serve you." The settlements were regarded as outposts of European ideas. Their Calvinism, so cheaply derided and so superficially understood, even to-day, was the intellectual platform of that portion of Europe which was mentally and morally awake to the vast issues involved in individual responsibility and self-government. Contemporary European democracy is hardly yet aware that Calvin's Institutes is one of its great charters. Continental Protestantism of the seventeenth century, like the militant Republicanism of the English Commonwealth, thus perused with fraternal interest the letters from Massachusetts Bay. And if Europe watched America in those days, it was no less true that America was watching Europe. Towards the end of the century, Cotton Mather, "prostrate in the dust" before the Lord, as his newly published Diary tells us, is wrestling "on the behalf of whole nations." He receives a "strong Persuasion that very overturning Dispensations of Heaven will quickly befal the French Empire"; he "lifts up his Cries for a mighty and speedy Revolution" there. "I spread before the Lord the Condition of His Church abroad ... especially in Great Britain and in France. And I prayed that the poor Vaudois may not be ruined by the Peace now made between France and Savoy. I prayed likewise for further Mortifications upon the Turkish Empire." Here surely was one colonial who was trying, in Cecil Rhodes's words, to "think continentally!"

Furthermore, the leaders of those early colonies were in large measure university men, disciplined in the classics, fit representatives of European culture. It has been reckoned that between the years 1630 and 1690 there were in New England as many graduates of Cambridge and Oxford as could be found in any population of similar size in the mother country. At one time during those years there was in Massachusetts and Connecticut alone a Cambridge graduate for every two hundred and fifty inhabitants. Like the exiled Greeks in Matthew Arnold's poem, they "undid their corded bales"—of learning, it is true, rather than of merchandise—upon these strange and inhospitable shores: and the traditions of Greek and

Hebrew and Latin scholarship were maintained with no loss of continuity. To the lover of letters there will always be something fine in the thought of that narrow seaboard fringe of faith in the classics, widening slowly as the wilderness gave way, making its invisible road up the rivers, across the mountains, into the great interior basin, and only after the Civil War finding an enduring home in the magnificent state universities of the West. Lovers of Greek and Roman literature may perhaps always feel themselves pilgrims and exiles in this vast industrial democracy of ours, but they have at least secured for us, and that from the very first day of the colonies, some of the best fruitage of internationalism. For that matter, what was, and is, that one Book—to the eyes of the Protestant seventeenth century infallible and inexpressively sacred—but the most potent and universal commerce of ideas and spirit, passing from the Orient, through Greek and Roman civilization, into the mind and heart of Western Europe and America?

"Oh, East is East, and West is West, And never the twain shall meet,"

declares a confident poet of to-day. But East and West met long ago in the matchless phrases translated from Hebrew and Greek and Latin into the English Bible; and the heart of the East there answers to the heart of the West as in water face answereth to face. That the colonizing Englishmen of the seventeenth century were Hebrews in spiritual culture, and heirs of Greece and Rome without ceasing to be Anglo-Saxon in blood, is one of the marvels of the history of civilization, and it is one of the basal facts in the intellectual life of the United States of to-day.

Yet that life, as I have already hinted, is not so simple in its terms as it might be if we had to reckon merely with the men of a single stock, albeit with imaginations quickened by contact with an Oriental religion, and minds disciplined, directly or indirectly, by the methods and the literatures which the Revival of Learning imposed upon modern Europe. American formal culture is, and has been, from the beginning, predominantly English. Yet it has been colored by the influences of other strains of race, and by alien intellectual traditions. Such international influences as have reached us through German and Scandinavian, Celtic and Italian, Russian and Jewish immigration, are well marked in certain localities, although their traces may be difficult to follow in the main trend of American writing. The presence of Negro, Irishman, Jew, and German, has affected our popular humor and satire, and is everywhere to be marked in the vocabulary and tone of our newspapers. The cosmopolitan character of the population of such cities as New York and Chicago strikes every foreign observer. Each one of the manifold races now transplanted here and in process of Americanization has for a while its own newspapers and churches and social life carried on in a foreign dialect. But this stage of evolution passes swiftly. The assimilative forces of American schools, industry, commerce, politics, are too strong for the foreign immigrant to resist. The Italian or Greek fruit pedler soon prefers to talk English, and his children can be made to talk nothing else. This extraordinary amalgamating power of English culture explains, no doubt, why German and Scandinavian immigration—to take examples from two of the most intelligent and educated races that have contributed to the up-building of the country—have left so little trace, as yet, upon our more permanent literature.

But blood will have its say sooner or later. No one knows how profoundly the strong mentality of the Jew, already evident enough in the fields of manufacturing and finance, will mould the intellectual life of the United States. The mere presence, to say nothing of the rapid absorption, of these millions upon millions of aliens, as the children of the Puritans regard them, is a constant evidence of the subtle ways in which internationalism is playing its part in the fashioning of the American temper. The moulding hand of the German university has been laid upon our higher institutions of learning for seventy years, although no one can demonstrate in set terms whether the influence of Goethe, read now by three generations of American scholars and studied by millions of youth in the schools, has left any real mark upon our literature. Abraham Lincoln, in his store-keeping days, used to sit under a tree outside the grocery store of Lincoln and Berry, reading Voltaire. One would like to think that he then and there assimilated something of the incomparable lucidity of style of the great Frenchman. But Voltaire's influence upon Lincoln's style cannot be proved, any more than Rousseau's direct influence upon Jefferson. Tolstoï and Ibsen have, indeed, left unmistakable traces upon American imaginative writing during the last quarter of a century. Frank Norris was indebted to Zola for the scheme of that uncompleted trilogy, the prose epic of the Wheat; and Owen Wister has revealed a not uncommon experience of our younger writing men in confessing that the impulse toward writing his Western stories came to him after reading the delightful pages of a French romancer. But all this tells us merely what we knew well enough before: that from colonial days to the present hour the Atlantic has been no insuperable barrier between the thought of Europe and the mind of America; that no one race bears aloft all the torches of intellectual progress; and that a really vital writer of any country finds a home in the spiritual life of every other country, even though it may be difficult to find his name in the local directory.

Finally, we must bear in mind that purely literary evidence as to the existence of certain national traits needs corroboration from many non-literary sources. If it is dangerous to judge modern Japan by the characteristics of a piece of pottery, it is only less misleading to select half a dozen excellent New England writers of fifty years ago as sole witnesses to the qualities of contemporary America. We must broaden the range of evidence. The historians of American literature must ultimately reckon with all those sources of mental and emotional quickening which have yielded to our pioneer people a substitute for purely literary pleasures: they must do justice to the immense mass of letters, diaries, sermons, editorials, speeches, which have served as the grammar and phrase-book of national feeling. A history of our literature must be flexible enough, as I have said elsewhere, to include "the social and economic and geographical background of American life; the zest of the explorer, the humor of the pioneer; the passion of old political battles; the yearning after spiritual truth and social readjustment; the baffled quest of beauty. Such a history must be broad enough for the Federalist and for Webster's oratory, for Beecher's sermons and Greeley's editorials, and the Lincoln-Douglas debates. It must picture the daily existence of our citizens from the beginning; their working ideas, their phrases and shibboleths and all their idols of the forum and the cave. It should portray the misspelled ideals of a profoundly idealistic people who have been usually immersed in material things."

Our most characteristic American writing, as must be pointed out again and again, is not the self-conscious literary performance of a Poe or a Hawthorne. It is civic writing; a citizen literature, produced, like the Federalist, and Garrison's editorials and Grant's Memoirs, without any stylistic consciousness whatever; a sort of writing which has been incidental to the accomplishment of some political, social, or moral purpose, and which scarcely regards itself as literature at all. The supreme example of it is the "Gettysburg Address." Homeliness, simplicity, directness, preoccupation with moral issues, have here been but the instrument of beauty; phrase and thought and feeling have a noble fitness to the national theme. "Nothing of Europe here," we may instinctively exclaim, and yet the profounder lesson of this citizen literature of ours is in the universality of the fundamental questions which our literature presents. The "Gettysburg Address" would not to-day have a secure fame in Europe if it spoke nothing to the ear and the heart of Europe. And this brings us back to our main theme. Lincoln, like Franklin, like many another lesser master of our citizen literature, is a typical American. In the writing produced by such men, there cannot but be a revelation of American characteristics. We are now to attempt an analysis of these national traits, as they have been expressed by our representative writers.

Simple as the problem seems, when thus stated, its adequate performance calls for a constant sensitiveness to the conditions prevalent, during a long period, in English and Continental society and literature. The most rudimentary biographical sketch of such eminent contemporary American authors as Mr. Henry James and Mr. Howells shows that Europe is an essential factor in the intellectual life and in the artistic procedure of these writers. Yet in their racial and national relationships they are indubitably American. In their local variations from type they demand from the critic an understanding of the culture of the Ohio Valley, and of Boston and New York. The analysis of the mingled racial, psychological, social, and professional traits in these masters of contemporary American fiction presents to the critic a problem as fascinating as, and I think more complex than, a corresponding study of Meredith or Hardy, of Daudet or D'Annunzio. In the three hundred years that have elapsed since Englishmen who were trained under Queen Elizabeth settled at Jamestown, Virginia, we have bred upon this soil many a master of speech. They have been men of varied gifts: now of clear intelligence, now of commanding power; men of rugged simplicity and of tantalizing subtlety; poets, novelists, orators, essayists, and publicists, who have interpreted the soul of America to the mind of the world. Our task is to exhibit the essential Americanism of these spokesmen of ours, to point out the traits which make them most truly representative of the instincts of the tongue-tied millions who work and plan and pass from sight without the gift and art of utterance; to find, in short, among the books which are recognized as constituting our American literature, some vital and illuminating illustrations of our national characteristics. For a truly "American" book — like an American national game, or an American city — is that which reveals, consciously or unconsciously, the American mind.

II

The American Mind

The origin of the phrase, "the American mind," was political. Shortly after the middle of the eighteenth century, there began to be a distinctly American way of regarding the debatable question of British Imperial control. During the period of the Stamp Act agitation our colonial-bred politicians and statesmen made the discovery that there was a mode of thinking and feeling which was native—or had by that time become a second nature—to all the colonists. Jefferson, for example, employs those resonant and useful words "the American mind" to indicate that throughout the American colonies an essential unity of opinion had been developed as regards the chief political question of the day.

It is one of the most striking characteristics of the present United States that this instinct of political unity should have endured, triumphing over every temporary motive of division. The inhabitants of the United States belong to a single political type. There is scarcely a news-stand in any country of Continental Europe where one may not purchase a newspaper openly or secretly opposed to the government,—not merely attacking an unpopular administration or minister or ruler,—but desiring and plotting the overthrow of the entire political system of the country. It is very difficult to find such a newspaper anywhere in the United States. I myself have never seen one. The opening sentence of President Butler's admirable little book, The American as He Is, originally delivered as lectures before the University of Copenhagen, runs as follows:

"The most impressive fact in American life is the substantial unity of view in regard to the fundamental questions of government and of conduct among a population so large, distributed over an area so wide, recruited from sources so many and so diverse, living under conditions so widely different."

But the American type of mind is evident in many other fields than that of politics. The stimulating book from which I have just quoted, attempts in its closing paragraph, after touching upon the more salient features of our national activity, to define the typical American in these words:—

"The typical American is he who, whether rich or poor, whether dwelling in the North, South, East, or West, whether scholar, professional man, merchant, manufacturer, farmer, or skilled worker for wages, lives the life of a good citizen and good neighbor; who believes loyally and with all his heart in his country's institutions, and in the underlying principles on which these institutions are built; who directs both his private and his public life by sound principles; who cherishes high ideals; and who aims to train his children for a useful life and for their country's service."

This modest and sensible statement indicates the existence of a national point of view. We have developed in the course of time, as a result of certain racial inheritances and historic experiences, a national "temper" or "ethos"; a more or less settled way of considering intellectual, moral, and social problems; in short, a peculiarly national attitude toward the universal human questions.

In a narrower sense, "the American mind" may mean the characteristics of the American intelligence, as it has been studied by Mr. Bryce, De Tocqueville, and other trained observers of our methods of thinking. It may mean the specific achievements of the American intelligence in fields like science and scholarship and history. In all these particular departments of intellectual activity the methods and the results of American workers have recently received expert and by no means uniformly favorable assessment from investigators upon both sides of the Atlantic. But the observer of literary processes and productions must necessarily take a somewhat broader survey of national tendencies. He must study what Nathaniel Hawthorne, with the instinct of a romance writer, preferred to call the "heart" as distinguished from the mere intellect. He must watch the moral and social and imaginative impulses of the individual; the desire for beauty; the hunger for self-expression; the conscious as well as the unconscious revelation of personality; and he must bring all this into relation—if he can, and knowing that the finer secrets are sure to elude him!—with the age-long impulses of the race and with the mysterious tides of feeling that flood or ebb with the changing fortunes of the nation.

One way to begin to understand the typical American is to take a look at him in Europe. It does not require a professional beggar or a licensed guide to identify him. Not that the American in Europe need recall in any particular the familiar pictorial caricature of "Uncle Sam." He need not bear any outward resemblances to such stage types as that presented in "The Man From Home." He need not even suggest, by peculiarities of speech or manner, that he has escaped from the pages of those novels of international observation in which Mr. James and Mr. Howells long ago attained an unmatched artistry. Our "American Abroad," at the present hour, may be studied without the aid of any literary recollections whatever. There he is, with his wife and daughters, and one may stare at him with all the frankness of a compatriot. He is obviously well-to-do,—else he would not be there at all,—and the wife and daughters seem very well-to-do indeed. He is kindly; considerate—sometimes effusively considerate—of his fellow travellers; patient with the ladies of his family, who in turn are noticeably patient with him. He is genial—very willing to talk with polyglot headwaiters and chauffeurs; in fact the wife and daughters are also practised conversationalists, although their most loyal admirers must admit that their voices are a trifle sharp or flat. These ladies are more widely read than "papa." He has not had much leisure for Ruskin and Symonds and Ferrero. His lack of historical training limits his curiosity concerning certain phases of his European surroundings; but he uses his eyes well upon such general objects as trains, hotel-service, and Englishmen. In spite of his habitual geniality, he is rather critical of foreign ways, although this is partly due to his lack of acquaintance with them. Intellectually, he is really more modest and self-distrustful than his conversation or perhaps his general bearing would imply; in fact, his wife and daughters, emboldened very likely by the training of their women's clubs, have a more commendable daring in assaulting new intellectual positions.

Yet the American does not lack quickness, either of wits or emotion. His humor and sentiment make him an entertaining companion. Even when his spirits run low, his patriotism is sure to mount in proportion, and he can always tell you with enthusiasm in just how many days he expects to be back again in what he calls "God's country."

This, or something like this, is the "American" whom the European regards with curiosity, contempt, admiration, or envy, as the case may be, but who is incontestably modifying Western Europe, even if he is not, as many journalists and globe-trotters are fond of asserting, "Americanizing" the world. Interesting as it is to glance at him against that European background which adds picturesqueness to his qualities, the "Man from Home" is still more interesting in his native habitat. There he has been visited by hundreds of curious and observant foreigners, who have left on record a whole literature of bewildered and bewildering, irritating and flattering and amusing testimony concerning the Americans. Settlers like Crèvecœur in the glowing dawn of the Republic, poets like Tom Moore, novelists like Charles Dickens, — other novelists like Mr. Arnold Bennett, — professional travellers like Captain Basil Hall, students of contemporary sociology like Paul Bourget and Mr. H. G. Wells, French journalists, German professors, Italian admirers of Colonel Roosevelt, political theorists like De Tocqueville, profound and friendly observers like Mr. Bryce, have had, and will continue to have, their say.

The reader who tries to take all this testimony at its face value, and to reconcile its contradictions, will be a candidate for the insane asylum. Yet the testimony is too amusing to be neglected and some of it is far too important to be ignored. Mr. John Graham Brooks, after long familiarity with these foreign opinions of America, has gathered some of the most representative of them into a delightful and stimulating volume entitled As Others See Us. There one may find examples of what the foreigner has seen, or imagined he has seen, during his sojourn in America, and what he has said about it afterwards. Mr. Brooks is too charitable to our visitors to quote the most fantastic and highly colored of their observations; but what remains is sufficiently bizarre.

The real service of such a volume is to train us in discounting the remarks made about us in a particular period like the eighteen-thirties, or from observations made in a special place, like Newport, or under special circumstances, like a Bishop's private car. It helps us to make allowances for the inevitable angle of nationality, the equally inevitable personal equation. A recent ambitious book on America, by a Washington journalist of long residence here, although of foreign birth, declares that "the chief trait of the American people is the love of gain and the desire of wealth acquired through commerce." That is the opinion of an expert observer, who has had extraordinary chances for seeing precisely what he has seen. I think it, notwithstanding, a preposterous opinion, fully as preposterous as Professor Muensterberg's notion that America has latterly grown more monarchical in its tendencies,—but I must remember that, in my own case, as in that of the journalist under consideration, there are allowances to be made for race, and training, and natural idiosyncracy of vision.

The native American, it may be well to remember, is something of an observer himself. If his observations upon the characteristics of his countrymen are less piquant than the foreigner's, it is chiefly because the American writes, upon the whole, less incisively than he talks. But incisive native writing about American traits is not lacking. If a missionary, say in South Africa, has read the New York Nationevery week for the past forty years, he has had an extraordinary "moving picture" of American tendencies, as interpreted by independent, trenchant, and high-minded criticism. That a file of the Nation will convey precisely the same impression of American tendencies as a file of the Sun, for instance, or the Boston Evening Transcript, is not to be affirmed. The humor of the London Punch and the New YorkLife does not differ more radically than the aspects of American civilization as viewed by two rival journals in Newspaper Row. The complexity of the material now collected and presented in daily journalism is so great that adequate editorial interpretation is obviously impossible. All the more insistently does this heterogeneous picture of American life demand the impartial interpretation of the historian, the imaginative transcription of the novelist. Humorist and moralist, preacher and mob orator and social essayist, shop-talk and talk over the tea-cup or over the pipe, and the far more illuminating instruction of events, are fashioning day by day the infinitely delicate processes of our national self-assessment. Scholars like Mr. Henry

Adams or Mr. James Ford Rhodes will explain to us American life as it was during the administrations of Jefferson or in the eighteen-fifties. Professor Turner will expound the significance of the frontier in American history. Mr. Henry James will portray with unrivalled psychological insight the Europeanized American of the eighteen-seventies and eighties. Literary critics like Professor Wendell or Professor Trent will deduce from our literature itself evidence concerning this or that national quality; and all this mass of American expert testimony, itself a result and a proof of national self-awareness and self-respect, must be put into the scales to balance, to confirm, or to outweigh the reports furnished by foreigners.

I do not pretend to be able, like an expert accountant, to draw up a balance-sheet of national qualities, to credit or debit the American character with this or that precise quantity of excellence or defect. But having turned the pages of many books about the United States,and listened to many conversations about its inhabitants in many states of the Union, I venture to collect a brief list of the qualities which have been assigned to us, together with a few, but not, I trust, too many, of our admitted national defects.

Like that excellent German who wrote the History of the English Drama in six volumes, I begin with Physical Geography. The differentiation of the physical characteristics of our branch of the English race is admittedly due, in part, to climate. In spite of the immense range of climatic variations as one passes from New England to New Orleans, from the Mississippi Valley to the high plains of the Far West, or from the rainy Oregon belt southward to San Diego, the settlers of English stock find a prevalent atmospheric condition, as a result of which they begin, in a generation or two, to change in physique. They grow thinner and more nervous, they "lean forward," as has been admirably said of them, while the Englishman "leans back"; they are less heavy and less steady; their voices are higher, sharper; their athletes get more easily "on edge"; they respond, in short, to an excessively stimulating climate. An old-fashioned sea-captain put it all into a sentence when he said that he could drink a bottle of wine with his dinner in Liverpool and only a half a bottle in New York. Explain the cause as we may, the fact seems to be that the body of John Bull changes, in the United States, into the body of Uncle Sam.

There are mental differences no less pronounced. No adjective has been more frequently applied to the Anglo-Saxon than the word "dull." The American mind has been accused of ignorance, superficiality, levity, commonplaceness, and dozens of other defects, but "dulness" is not one of them. "Smartness," rather, is the preferred epithet of derogation; or, to rise a little in the scale of valuation, it is the word "cleverness," used with that lurking contempt for cleverness which is truly English and which long survived in the dialect of New England, where the village ne'er-do-well or Jack-of-all-trades used to be pronounced a "clever" fellow. The variety of employments to which the American pioneers were obliged to betake themselves has done something, no doubt, to produce a national versatility, a quick assimilation of new methods and notions, a ready adaptability to novel emergencies. An invaluable pioneer trait is curiosity; the settler in a new country, like Moses in the wilderness of Arabia, must "turn aside to see"; he must look into things, learn to read signs, — or else the Indians or frost or freshet will soon put an end to his pioneering. That curiosity concerning strangers which so much irritated Dickens and Mrs. Trollope was natural to the children of Western emigrants to whom the difference between Sioux and Pawnee had once meant life or death. "What's your business, stranger, in these parts?" was an instinctive, because it had once been a vital, question. That it degenerates into mere inquisitiveness is true enough; just as the "acuteness," the "awareness," essential to the existence of one generation becomes only "cuteness," the typical tin-pedler's habit of mind, in the generation following.

American inexperience, the national rawness and unsophistication which has impressed so many observers, has likewise its double significance when viewed historically. We have exhibited, no doubt, the amateurishness and recklessness which spring from relative isolation, from ignorance as to how they manage elsewhere this particular sort of thing, — the conservation of forests, let us say, or the government of colonial dependencies. National smugness and conceit, the impatience crystallized in the phrase, "What have we got to do with abroad?" have jarred upon the nerves of many cultivated Americans. But it is no less true that a nation of pioneers and settlers, like the isolated individual, learns certain rough-and-ready Robinson Crusoe ways of getting things done. A California mining-camp is sure to establish law and order in due time, though never, perhaps, a law and order quite according to Blackstone. In the most trying crises of American political history, it was not, after all, a question of profiting by European experience. Washington and Lincoln, in their sorest struggles, had nothing to do with "abroad"; the problem had first to be thought through, and then fought through, in American and not in European terms. Not a half-dozen Englishmen understood the bearings of the Kansas-Nebraska Bill, or, if they did, we were little the wiser. We had to wait until a slow-minded frontier lawyer mastered it in all its implications, and then patiently explained it to the farmers of Illinois, to the United States, and to the world.

It is true that the unsophisticated mode of procedure may turn out to be sheer folly,—a "sixteen to one" triumph of provincial barbarism. But sometimes it is the secret of freshness and of force. Your cross-country runner scorns the highway, but that is because he has confidence in his legs and loins, and he likes to take the fences. Fenimore Cooper, when he began to write stories, knew nothing about the art of novel-making as practised in Europe, but he possessed something infinitely better for him, namely, instinct, and he took the right road to the climax of a narrative as unerringly as the homing bee follows its viewless trail.

No one can be unaware how easily this superb American confidence may turn to over-confidence, to sheer recklessness. We love to run past the signals, in our railroading and in our thinking. Emerson will "plunge" on a new idea as serenely as any stock-gambler ever "plunged" in Wall Street, and a pretty school-teacher will tell you that she has become an advocate of the "New Thought" as complacently as an old financier will boast of having bought Calumet and Hecla when it was selling at 25. (Perhaps the school-teacher may get as good a bargain. I cannot say.) Upon the whole, Americans back individual guesswork and pay cheerfully when they lose.

A great many of them, as it happens, have guessed right. Even those who continue to guess wrong, like Colonel Sellers, have the indefeasible romantic appetite for guessing again. The American temperament and the chances of American history have brought constant temptation to speculation, and plenty of our people prefer to gamble upon what they love to call a "proposition," rather than to go to the bottom of the facts. They would rather speculate than know.

Doubtless there are purely physical causes that have encouraged this mental attitude, such as the apparently inexhaustible resources of a newly opened country, the consciousness of youthful energy, the feeling that any very radical mistake in pitching camp to-day can easily be rectified when we pitch camp to-morrow. The habit of exaggeration which was so particularly annoying to English visitors in the middle of the last century — annoying even to Charles Dickens, who was himself something of an expert in exuberance — is a physical and moral no less than a mental quality. That monstrous braggadocio which Dickens properly satirized in Martin Chuzzlewit was partly, of course, the product of provincial ignorance. Doubtless there were, and there are still, plenty of Pograms who are convinced that Henry Clay and Daniel Webster overtop all the intellectual giants of the Old World. But that youthful bragging, and perhaps some of the later bragging as well, has its social side. It is a perverted idealism. It springs from group loyalty, from sectional fidelity. The settlement of "Eden" may be precisely what Dickens drew it: a miasmatic mud-hole. Yet we who are interested in the new town do not intend, as the popular phrase has it, "to give ourselves away." We back our own "proposition," so that to this day Chicago cannot tell the truth to St. Louis, nor Harvard to Yale. Braggadocio thus gets glorified through its rootage in loyalty; and likewise extravagance — surely one of the worst of American mental vices — is often based upon a romantic confidence in individual opinion or in the righteousness of some specific cause. Convince a blue-blooded American like Wendell Phillips that the abolition of slavery is right, and, straightway, words and even facts become to him mere weapons in a splendid warfare. His statements grow rhetorical, reckless, virulent. Proof seems to him, as it did to the contemporary

Transcendentalist philosophers, an impertinence. The sole question is, "Are you on the Lord's side?" i.e., on the side of Wendell Phillips.

Excuse as we may the faults of a gifted combatant in a moral crisis like the abolition controversy, the fact remains that the intellectual dangers of the oratorical temperament are typically American. What is commonly called our "Fourth of July" period has indeed passed away. It has few apologists, perhaps fewer than it really deserves. It is possible to regret the disappearance of that old-fashioned assertion of patriotism and pride, and to question whether historical pageants and a "noiseless Fourth" will develop any better citizens than the fathers were. But on the purely intellectual side, the influence of that spread-eagle oratory was disastrous. Throughout wide-extended regions of the country, and particularly in the South and West, the "orator" grew to be, in the popular mind, the normal representative of intellectual ability. Words, rather than things, climbed into the saddle. Popular assemblies were taught the vocabulary and the logic of passion, rather than of sober, lucid reasoning. The "stump" grew more potent than school-house and church and bench; and it taught its reckless and passionate ways to more than one generation. The intellectual leaders of the newer South have more than once suffered ostracism for protesting against this glorification of mere oratory. But it is not the South alone that has suffered. Wherever a mob can gather, there are still the dangers of the old demagogic vocabulary and rhetoric. The mob state of mind is lurking still in the excitable American temperament.

The intellectual temptations of that temperament are revealed no less in our popular journalism. This journalism, it is needless to say, is extremely able, but it is reckless to the last degree. The extravagance of its head-lines and the over-statements of its news columns are direct sources of profit, since they increase the circulation and it is circulation which wins advertising space. I think it is fair to say that the American people, as a whole, like precisely the sort of journalism which they get. The tastes of the dwellers in cities control, more and more, the character of our newspapers. The journals of New York, Chicago, and San Francisco are steadily gaining in circulation, in resourcefulness, and in public spirit, but they are, for the most part, unscrupulous in attack, sophistical, and passionate. They outvie the popular pulpit in sentimentality. They play with fire.

The note of exaggeration which is heard in American oratory and journalism is struck again in the popular magazines. Their campaign of "exposure," during the last decade, has been careless of individual and corporate rights and reputations. Even the magazine sketches and short stories are keyed up to a hysteric pitch. So universally is this characteristic national tension displayed in our periodical literature that no one is much surprised to read in his morning paper that some one has called the President of the United States a liar, — or that some one has been called a liar by the President of the United States.

For an explanation of these defects, shall we fall back upon a convenient maxim of De Tocqueville's and admit with him that "a democracy is unsuited to meditation"? We are forced to do so. But then comes the inevitable second thought that a democracy must needs have other things than meditation to attend to. Athenian and Florentine and Versailles types of political despotism have all proved highly favorable to the lucubrations of philosophers and men of letters who enjoyed the despot's approbation. For that matter, no scheme of life was ever better suited to meditation than an Indian reservation in the eighteen-seventies, with a Great Father in Washington to furnish blankets, flour, and tobacco. Yet that is not quite the American ideal of existence, and it even failed to produce the peaceable fruits of meditation in the Indian himself.

One may freely admit the shortcomings of the American intelligence; the "commonness of mind and tone" which Mr. Bryce believes to be inseparable from the presence of such masses of men associated under modern democratic government; the frivolity and extravagance which represent the gasconading of the romantic temper in face of the grey practicalities of everyday routine; the provincial boastfulness and bad taste which have resulted from intellectual isolation; the lack, in short, of a code, whether for thought or speech or behavior. And nevertheless, one's instinctive Americanism replies, May it not be better, after all, to have gone without a code for a while, to have lacked that orderly and methodized and socialized European intelligence, and to have had the glorious sense of bringing things to pass in spite of it? There is just one thing that would have been fatal to our democracy. It is the feeling expressed in La Bruyère's famous book: "Everything has been said, everything has been written, everything has been done." Here in America everything was to do; we were forced to conjugate our verbs in the future tense. No doubt our existence has been, in some respects, one of barbarism, but it has been the barbarism of life and not of death. A rawboned baby sprawling on the mud floor of a Kentucky log cabin is a more hopeful spectacle than a wholly civilized funeral.

"Perhaps it is," rejoins the European critic, somewhat impatiently, "but you are confusing the issue. We find certain grave defects in the American mind, defects which, if you had not had what Thomas Carlyle called 'a great deal of land for a very few people,' would long ago have involved you in disaster. You admit the mental defects, but you promptly shift the question to one of moral qualities, of practical energy, of subduing your wilderness, and so forth. You have too often absented yourself from the wedding banquet, from the European symposium of wit and philosophy, from the polished and orderly and delightful play and interplay of civilized mind,—and your excuse is the old one: that you are trying your yoke of oxen and cannot come. We charge you with intellectual sins, and you enter the plea of moral preoccupation. If you will permit personal examples, you Americans have made ere now your national heroes out of men whose reasoning powers remained those of a college sophomore, who were unable to state an opponent's position with fairness, who lacked wholly the judicial quality, who were vainglorious and extravagant, who had, in short, the mind of an exuberant barbarian; but you instantly forget their intellectual defects in the presence of their abounding physical and moral energy, their freedom from any taint of personal corruption, their whole-souled desire and effort for the public good. Were not such heroes, impossible as they would have been in any other civilized country, perfectly illuminative of your national state of mind?"

For one, I confess that I do not know what reply to make to my imaginary European critic. I suspect that he is right. At any rate, we stand here at the fork of the road. If we do not wish to linger any longer over a catalogue of intellectual sins, let us turn frankly to our moral preoccupations, comforting ourselves, if we like, as we abandon the field of purely intellectual rivalry with Europe, in the reflection that it is the muddle-headed Anglo-Saxon, after all, who is the dominant force in the modern world.

The moral temper of the American people has been analyzed no less frequently than their mental traits. Foreign and native observers are alike agreed in their recognition of the extraordinary American energy. The sheer power of the American bodily machine, driven by the American will, is magnificent. It is often driven too hard, and with reckless disregard of anything save immediate results. It wears out more quickly than the bodily machine of the Englishman. It is typical that the best distance runners of Great Britain usually beat ours, while we beat them in the sprints. Our public men are frequently — as the athletes say — "all in" at sixty. Their energy is exhausted at just the time that many an English statesman begins his best public service. But after making every allowance for wasteful excess, for the restless and impatient consumption of nervous forces which nature intended that we should hold in reserve, the fact remains that American history has demonstrated the existence of a dynamic national energy, physical and moral, which is still unabated. Immigration has turned hitherward the feet of millions upon millions of young men from the hardiest stocks of Europe. They replenish the slackening streams of vigor. When the northern New Englander cannot make a living on the old farm, the French Canadian takes it off his hands, and not only improves the farm, but raises big crops of boys. So with Italians, Swedes, Germans, Irish, Jews, and Portuguese, and all the rest. We are a nation of immigrants, a digging, hewing, building, breeding, bettering race, of mixed blood and varying creeds, but of fundamental faith in the wages of going on; a race compounded of materials crude but potent; raw, but with blood that is red and bones that are big; a race that is accomplishing its vital tasks, and, little by little, transmuting brute forces and material energies into the finer play of mind and spirit.

From the very beginning, the American people have been characterized by idealism. It was the inner light of Pilgrim and Quaker colonists; it gleams no less in the faces of the children of Russian Jew immigrants to-day. American irreverence has been noted by many a foreign critic, but there are certain subjects in whose presence our reckless or cynical speech is hushed. Compared with current Continental humor, our characteristic American humor is peculiarly reverent. The purity of woman and the reality of religion are not considered topics for jocosity. Cleanness of body and of mind are held by our young men to be not only desirable but attainable virtues. There is among us, in comparison with France or Germany, a defective reverence for the State as such; and a positive irreverence towards the laws of the Commonwealth, and towards the occupants of high political positions. Mayor, Judge, Governor, Senator, or even President, may be the butt of such indecorous ridicule as shocks or disgusts the foreigner; but nevertheless the personal joke stops short of certain topics which Puritan tradition disapproves. The United States is properly called a Christian nation, not merely because the Supreme Court has so affirmed it, but because the phrase "a Christian nation" expresses the historical form which the religious idealism of the country has made its own. The Bible is still considered, by the mass of the people, a sacred book; oaths in courts of law, oaths of persons elected to great office, are administered upon it. American faith in education, as all the world knows, has from the beginning gone hand in hand with faith in religion; the school-house was almost as sacred a symbol as the meeting-house; and the munificence of American private benefactions to the cause of education furnishes to-day one of the most striking instances of idealism in the history of civilization.

The ideal passions of patriotism, of liberty, of loyalty to home and section, of humanitarian and missionary effort, have all burned with a clear flame in the United States. The optimism which lies so deeply embedded in the American character is one phase of the national mind. Charles Eliot Norton once said to me, with his dry humor, that there was an infallible test of the American authorship of any anonymous article or essay: "Does it contain the phrase 'After all, we need not despair'? If it does, it was written by an American." In spite of all that is said about the practicality of the American, his love of gain and his absorption in material interests, those who really know him are aware how habitually he confronts his practical tasks in a spirit of romantic enthusiasm. He marches downtown to his prosaic day's job and calls it "playing the game"; to work as hard as he can is to "get into the game," and to work as long as he can is to "stay in the game"; he loves to win fully as much as the Jew and he hates to lose fully as much as the Englishman, but losing or winning, he carries into his business activity the mood of the idealist.

It is easy to think of all this as self-deception as the emotional effusiveness of the American temperament; but to refuse to see its idealism is to mistake fundamentally the character of the American man. No doubt he does deceive himself often as to his real motives: he is a mystic and a bargain-hunter by turns. Divided aims, confused ideals, have struggled for the mastery among us, ever since Challon'sVoyage, in 1606, announced that the purpose of the first colonists to Virginia was "both to seek to convert the savages, as also to seek out what benefits or commodities might be had in those parts." How that "both"—"as also" keeps echoing in American history: "both" to christianize the Negro and work him at a profit, "both" duty and advantage in retaining the Philippines; "both" international good will and increased armaments; "both" Sunday morning precepts and Monday morning practice; "both" horns of a dilemma; "both God and mammon"; did ever a nation possess a more marvellous water-tight compartment method of believing and honoring opposites! But in all this unconscious hypocrisy the American is perhaps not worse—though he may be more absurd!—than other men.

Another aspect of the American mind is found in our radicalism. "To be an American," it has been declared, "is to be a radical." That statement needs qualification. Intellectually the American is inclined to radical views; he is willing to push certain social theories very far; he will found a new religion, a new philosophy, a new socialistic community, at the slightest notice or provocation; but he has at bottom a fund of moral and political conservatism. Thomas Jefferson, one of the greatest of our radical idealists, had a good deal of the English squire in him after all. Jeffersonianism endures, not merely because it is a radical theory of human nature, but because it expresses certain facts of human nature. The American mind looks forward, not back; but in practical details of land, taxes, and governmental machinery we are instinctively cautious of change. The State of Connecticut knows that her constitution is ill adapted to the present conditions of her population, but the difficulty is to persuade the rural legislators to amend it. Yet everybody admits that amendment will come "some day." This admission is a characteristic note of American feeling; and every now and then come what we call "uplift" movements, when radicalism is in the very air, and a thousand good "causes" take fresh vigor.

One such period was in the New England of the eighteen-forties. We are moving in a similar—only this time a national—current of radicalism, to-day. But a change in the weather or the crops has before now turned many of our citizens from radicalism into conservatism. There is, in fact, conservatism in our blood and radicalism in our brains, and now one and now the other rules. Very typical of American radicalism is that story of the old sea-captain who was ignorant, as was supposed, of the science of navigation, and who cheerfully defended himself by saying that he could work his vessel down to Boston Light without knowing any navigation, and after that he could go where he "dum pleased." I suspect the old fellow pulled his sextant and chronometer out of his chest as soon as he really needed them. American radicalism is not always as innocent of the world's experience as it looks. In fact, one of the most interesting phases of this twentieth century "uplift" movement is its respect and even glorification of expert opinion. A German expert in city-planning electrifies an audience of Chicago club-women by talking to them about drains, ash-carts, and flower-beds. A hundred other experts, in sanitation, hygiene, chemistry, conservation of natural resources, government by commission, tariffs, arbitration treaties, are talking quite as busily; and they have the attention of a national audience that is listening with genuine modesty, and with a real desire to refashion American life on wiser and nobler plans. In this national forward movement in which we are living, radicalism has shown its beneficent aspect of constructive idealism.

No catalogue of American qualities and defects can exclude the trait of individualism. We exalt character over institutions, says Mr. Brownell; we like our institutions because they suit us, and not because we admire institutions. "Produce great persons," declares Walt Whitman, "the rest follows." Whether the rest follows or not, there can be no question that Americans, from the beginning, have laid singular stress upon personal qualities. The religion and philosophy of the Puritans were in this respect at one with the gospel of the frontier. It was the principle of "every man for himself"; solitary confrontation of his God, solitary struggle with the wilderness. "He that will not work," declared John Smith after that first disastrous winter at Jamestown, "neither let him eat." The pioneer must clear his own land, harvest his own crops, defend his own fireside; his temporal and eternal salvation were strictly his own affair. He asked, and expected, no aid from the community; he could at most "change works" in time of harvest, with a neighbor, if he had one. It was the sternest school of self-reliance, from babyhood to the grave, that human society is ever likely to witness. It bred heroes and cranks and hermits; its glories and its eccentricities are written in the pages of Emerson, Thoreau, and Whitman; they are written more permanently still in the instinctive American faith in individual manhood. Our democracy idolizes a few individuals; it ignores their defective training, or, it may be, their defective culture; it likes to think of an Andrew Jackson who was a "lawyer, judge, planter, merchant, general, and politician," before he became President; it asks only that the man shall not change his individual character in passing from one occupation or position to another; in fact, it is amused and proud to think of Grant hauling cordwood to market, of Lincoln keeping store or Roosevelt rounding-up cattle. The one essential question was put by Hawthorne into the mouth of Holgrave in the House of the Seven Gables. Holgrave had been by turns a schoolmaster, clerk in a store, editor, pedler, lecturer on Mesmerism, and daguerreotypist, but "amid all these personal vicissitudes," says Hawthorne, "he had never lost his identity.... He had never violated the innermost man, but had carried his conscience along with him." There speaks the local accent of Puritanism, but the voice insisting upon the moral integrity of the individual is the undertone of America.

Finally, and surely not the least notable of American traits, is public spirit. Triumphant individualism checks itself, or is rudely checked in spite of itself, by considerations of the general good. How often have French critics confessed, with humiliation, that in spite of the superior socialization of the French intelligence, France has yet to learn from America the art and habit of devoting individual fortunes to the good of the community. Our American literature, as has been already pointed out, is characteristically a citizen literature, responsive to the civic note, the production of men who, like the writers of the Federalist, applied a vigorous practical intelligence, a robust common sense, to questions affecting the interest of everybody. The spirit of fair play in our free democracy has led Americans to ask not merely what is right and just for one, the individual, but what are righteousness and justice and fair play for all. Democracy, as embodied in such a leader as Lincoln, has meant Fellowship. Nothing finer can be said of a representative American than to say of him, as Mr. Norton said of Mr. Lowell, that he had a "most public soul."

No one can present such a catalogue of American qualities as I have attempted without realizing how much escapes his classification. Conscious criticism and assessment of national characteristics is essential to an understanding of them; but one feels somehow that the net is not holding. The analysis of English racial inheritances, as modified by historical conditions, yields much, no doubt; but what are we to say of such magnificent embodiments of the American spirit as are revealed in the Swiss immigrant Agassiz, the German exile Carl Schurz, the native-born mulatto Booker Washington? The Americanism of representative Americans is something which must be felt; it is to be reached by imaginative perception and sympathy, no less than by the process of formal analysis. It would puzzle the experts in racial tendencies to find arithmetically the common denominator of such American figures as

Franklin, Washington, Jackson, Webster, Lee, Lincoln, Emerson, and "Mark Twain"; yet the countrymen of those typical Americans instinctively recognize in them a sort of largeness, genuineness, naturalness, kindliness, humor, effectiveness, idealism, which are indubitably and fundamentally American.

There are certain sentiments of which we ourselves are conscious, though we can scarcely translate them into words, and these vaguely felt emotions of admiration, of effort, of fellowship and social faith are the invisible America. Take, for a single example, the national admiration for what we call a "self-made" man: here is a boy selling candy and newspapers on a Michigan Central train; he makes up his mind to be a lawyer; in twelve years from that day he is general counsel for the Michigan Central road; he enters the Senate of the United States and becomes one of its leading figures. The instinctive flush of sympathy and pride with which Americans listen to such a story is far more deeply based than any vulgar admiration for money-making abilities. No one cares whether such a man is rich or poor. He has vindicated anew the possibilities of manhood under American conditions of opportunity; the miracle of our faith has in him come true once more.

No one can understand America with his brains. It is too big, too puzzling. It tempts, and it deceives. But many an illiterate immigrant has felt the true America in his pulses before he ever crossed the Atlantic. The descendant of the Pilgrims still remains ignorant of our national life if he does not respond to its glorious zest, its throbbing energy, its forward urge, its uncomprehending belief in the future, its sense of the fresh and mighty world just beyond to-day's horizon. Whitman's "Pioneers, O Pioneers" is one of the truest of American poems because it beats with the pulse of this onward movement, because it is full of this laughing and conquering fellowship and of undefeated faith.

III

American Idealism

Our endeavor to state the general characteristics of the American mind has already given us some indication of what Americans really care for. The things or the qualities which they like, the objects of their conscious or unconscious striving, are their ideals. "There is what I call the American idea," said Theodore Parker in the Anti-Slavery Convention of 1850. "This idea demands, as the proximate organization thereof, a democracy — that is, a government of all the people, by all the people, for all the people; of course, a government on the principle of eternal justice, the unchanging law of God; for shortness' sake, I will call it the idea of Freedom." That is one of a thousand definitions of American idealism. Books devoted to the "Spirit of America" — like the volume by Henry van Dyke which bears that very title — give a programme of national accomplishments and aspirations. But our immediate task is more specific. It is to point out how adequately this idealistic side of the national temperament has been expressed in American writing. Has our literature kept equal pace with our thinking and feeling?

We do not need, in attempting to answer this question, any definition of idealism, in its philosophical or in its more purely literary sense. There are certain fundamental human sentiments which lift men above brutes, Frenchmen above "frog-eaters," and Englishmen above "shop-keepers." These ennobling sentiments or ideals, while universal in their essential nature, assume in each civilized nation a somewhat specific coloring. The national literature reveals the myriad shades and hues of private and public feeling, and the more truthful this literary record, the more delicate and noble become the harmonies of local and national thought or emotion with the universal instincts and passions of mankind. On the other hand, when the literature of Spain, for instance, or of Italy, fails, within a given period, in range and depth of human interest, we are compelled to believe either that the Spain or Italy of that age was wanting in the nobler ideals, or that it lacked literary interpretation.

In the case of America we are confronted by a similar dilemma. Since the beginning of the seventeenth century this country has been, in a peculiar sense, the home of idealism; but our literature has remained through long periods thin and provincial, barren in cosmopolitan significance; and the hard fact faces us to-day that only three or four of our writers have aroused any strong interest in the cultivated readers of continental Europe. Evidently, then, either the torch of American idealism does not burn as brightly as we think, or else our writers, with but few exceptions, have not hitherto possessed the height and reach and grasp to hold up the torch so that the world could see it. Let us look first at the flame, and then at the torch-bearers.

Readers of Carlyle have often been touched by the humility with which that disinherited child of Calvinism speaks of Goethe's doctrine of the "Three Reverences," as set forth in Wilhelm Meister. Again and again, in his correspondence and his essays, does Carlyle recur to that teaching of the threefold Reverence: Reverence for what is above us, for what is around us and for what is under us; that is to say, the ethnic religion which frees us from debasing fear, the philosophical religion which unites us with our comrades, and the Christian religion which recognizes humility and poverty and suffering as divine.

"To which of these religions do you specially adhere?" inquired Wilhelm.

"To all the three," replied the sages; "for in their union they produce what may properly be called the true Religion. Out of those three Reverences springs the highest Reverence, Reverence for Oneself."

An admirable symbolism, surely; vaguer, no doubt, than the old symbols which Carlyle had learned in the Kirk at Ecclefechan, but less vague, in turn, than that doctrine of reverence for the Oversoul, which was soon to be taught at Concord.

As one meditates upon the idealism of the first colonists in America, one is tempted to ask what their "reverences" were. Toward what tangible symbols of the invisible did their eyes instinctively turn?

For New England, at least, the answer is relatively simple. One form of it is contained in John Adams's well-known prescription for Virginia, as recorded in his Diary for July 21, 1786. "Major Langbourne dined with us again. He was lamenting the difference of character between Virginia and New England. I offered to give him a receipt for making a New England in Virginia. He desired it; and I recommended to him town-meetings, training-days, town-schools, and ministers."

The "ministers," it will be noticed, come last on the Adams list. But the order of precedence is unimportant.

Here are four symbols, or, if you like, "reverences." Might not the Virginia planters, loyal to their own specific symbol of the "gentleman,"—no unworthy ideal, surely; one that had been glorified in European literature ever since Castiligione wrote his Courtier, and one that had been transplanted from England to Virginia as soon as Sir Walter Raleigh's men set foot on the soil which took its name from the Virgin Queen,—might not the Virginia gentlemen have pondered to their profit over the blunt suggestion of the Massachusetts commoner? No doubt; and yet how much picturesqueness and nobility—and tragedy, too—we should have missed, if our history had not been full of these varying symbols, clashing ideals, different Reverences!

One Reverence, at least, was common to the Englishman of Virginia and to the Englishman of Plymouth and Massachusetts Bay. They were joint heirs of the Reformation, children of that waxing and puissant England which was a nation of one book, the Bible; a book whose phrases color alike the Faerie Queen of Spenser and the essays of Francis Bacon; a book rich beyond all others in human experience; full of poetry, history, drama; the test of conduct; the manual of devotion; and above all, and blinding all other considerations by the very splendor of the thought, a book believed to be the veritable Word of the unseen God. For these colonists in the wilderness, as for the Protestant Europe which they had left irrevocably behind them, the Bible was the plainest of all symbols of idealism: it was the first of the "Reverences."

The Church was a symbol likewise, but to the greater portion of colonial America the Church meant chiefly the tangible band of militant believers within the limits of a certain township or parish, rather than the mystical Bride of Christ. Except in Maryland and Virginia, whither the older forms of Church worship were early transplanted, there was scanty reverence for the Establishment. There was neither clergyman nor minister on board the Mayflower. In Rufus Choate's oration on the Pilgrims before the New England Society of New York in 1843, occurred the famous sentence about "a church without a bishop and a state without a King"; to which Dr. Wainwright, rector of St. John's, replied wittily at the dinner following the oration that there "can be no church without a bishop." This is perhaps a question for experts; but Thomas Hooker, Thomas Shepard, and John Cotton would have sided with Rufus Choate. The awe which had once been paid to the Establishment was transferred, in the seventeenth-century New England, to the minister. The minister imposed himself upon the popular imagination, partly through sheer force of personal ascendency, and partly as a symbol of the theocracy,—the actual governing of the Commonwealth by the laws and spirit of the sterner Scriptures. The minister dwelt apart as upon an awful Sinai. It was no mere romantic fancy of Hawthorne that shadowed his countenance with a black veil. The church organization, too,—though it may have lacked its bishop,—had a despotic power over its communicants; to be cast out of its fellowship involved social and political consequences comparable to those following excommunication by the Church of Rome. Hawthorne and Whittier and Longfellow—all of them sound antiquarians, though none of them in sympathy with the theology of Puritanism—have described in fit terms the bareness of the New England meeting-house. What intellectual severity and strain was there; what prodigality of learning; what blazing intensity of devotion; what pathos of women's patience, and of children, prematurely old, stretched upon the rack of insoluble problems! What dramas of the soul were played through to the end in those barn-like buildings, where the musket, perhaps, stood in the corner of the pew! "How aweful is this place!" must have been murmured by the lips of all; though there were many who have added, "This is the gate of Heaven."

The gentler side of colonial religion is winningly portrayed in Whittier's Pennsylvania Pilgrim and in his imaginary journal of Margaret Smith. There were sunnier slopes, warmer exposures for the ripening of the human spirit, in the Southern colonies. Even in New England there was sporadic revolt from the beginning. The number of non-church-members increased rapidly after 1700; Franklin as a youth in Boston admired Cotton Mather's ability, but he did not go to church, "Sunday being my studying day." Doubtless there were always humorous sceptics like Mrs. Stowe's delightful Sam Lawson in Oldtown Folks. Lawson's comment on Parson Simpson's service epitomizes two centuries of New England thinking. "Wal," said Sam, "Parson Simpson's a smart man; but I tell ye, it's kind o' discouragin'. Why, he said our state and condition by natur was just like this. We was clear down in a well fifty feet deep, and the sides all round nothin' but glare ice; but we was under immediate obligations to get out, 'cause we was free, voluntary agents. But nobody ever had got out, and nobody would, unless the Lord reached down and took 'em. And whether he would or not nobody could tell; it was all sovereignty. He said there wan't one in a hundred, not one in a thousand,—not one in ten thousand,—that would be saved. Lordy massy, says I to myself, ef that's so they're any of 'em welcome to my chance. And so I kind o' ris up and come out."

Mrs. Stowe's novel is fairly representative of a great mass of derivative literature which draws its materials from the meeting-house period of American history. But the direct literature of that period has passed almost wholly into oblivion. Jonathan Edwards had one of the finest minds of his century; no European standard of comparison is too high for him; he belongs with Pascal, with Augustine, if you like, with Dante. But his great treatises written in the Stockbridge woods are known only to a few technical students of philosophy. One terrible sermon, preached at Enfield in 1741, is still read by the curious; but scarcely anybody knows of the ineffable tenderness, dignity, and pathos of his farewell sermon to his flock at Northampton: and the Yale Library possesses nearly twelve hundred of Edwards's sermons which have never been printed at all. Nor does anybody, save here and there an antiquarian, read Shepard and Hooker and Mayhew. And yet these preachers and their successors furnished the emotional equivalents of great prose and verse to generations of men. "That is poetry," says Professor Saintsbury (in a dangerous latitudinarianism, perhaps!), "which gives the reader the feeling of poetry." Here we touch one of the fundamental characteristics of our national state of mind, in its relation to literature. We are careless of form and type, yet we crave the emotional stimulus. Milton, greatest of Puritan poets, was read and quoted all too seldom in the Puritan colonies, and yet those colonists were no strangers to the emotions of sublimity and awe and beauty. They found them in the meeting-house instead of in a book; precisely as, in a later day, millions of Americans experienced what was for them the emotional equivalent of poetry in the sermons of Henry Ward Beecher and Phillips Brooks. French pulpit oratory of the seventeenth century wins recognition as a distinct type of literature; its great practitioners, like Massillon, Bourdaloue, Bossuet, are appraised in all the histories of the national literature and in books devoted to the evolution of literary species. In the American colonies the great preachers performed the functions of men of letters without knowing it. They have been treated with too scant respect in the histories of American literature. It is one of the penalties of Protestantism that the audiences, after a while, outgrow the preacher. The development of the historic sense, of criticism, of science, makes an impassable gulf between Jonathan Edwards and the American churches of the twentieth century. A sense of profound changes in theology has left our contemporaries indifferent to the literature in which the old theology was clothed.

There is one department of American literary production, of which Bossuet's famous sermon on Queen Henrietta Maria of England may serve to remind us, which illustrates significantly the national idealism. I mean the commemorative oration. The addresses upon the Pilgrim Fathers by such orators as Everett, Webster, and Choate; the countless orations before such organizations as the New England Society of New York and the Phi Beta Kappa; the papers read before historical and patriotic societies; the birthday and centenary discourses upon national figures like Washington or Lincoln, have all performed, and are still performing, an inestimable service in stimulating popular loyalty to the idealism of the fathers. As literature, most of this production is derivative: we listen to eloquence about the Puritans, but we do not read the Puritans; the description of Arthur Dimmesdale's election sermon in The Scarlet Letter, moving as it may be, tempts no one to open the stout collections of election sermons in the libraries. Yet the original literature of mediæval chivalry is known only to a few scholars: Tennyson's Idylls outsell the Mabinogion and Malory. The actual world of literature is always shop-worn; a world chiefly of second-hand books, of warmed-over emotions and it is not surprising that many listeners to orations about Lincoln do not personally emulate Lincoln, and that many of the most enthusiastic dealers in the sentiment of the ancestral meeting-house do not themselves attend church.

The other ingredients of John Adams's ideal Commonwealth are no less significant of our national disposition. Take the school-house. It was planted in the wilderness for the training of boys and girls and for a future "godly and learned ministry." The record of American education is a long story of idealism which has touched literature at every turn. The "red school-house" on the hill-top or at the cross-roads, the "log-colleges" in forgotten hamlets, the universities founded by great states, are all a record of the American faith—which has sometimes been called a fetich—in education. In its origin, it was a part of the essential programme of Calvinism to make a man able to judge for himself upon the most momentous questions; a programme, too, of that political democracy which lay embedded in the tenets of Calvinism, a democracy which believes and must continue to believe that an educated electorate can safeguard its own interests and train up its own leaders. The poetry of the American school-house was written long ago by Whittier, in describing Joshua Coffin's school under the big elm on the cross-road in East Haverhill; its humor and pathos and drama have been portrayed by innumerable story-writers and essayists. Mrs. Martha Baker Dunn's charming sketches, entitled "Cicero in Maine" and "Virgil in Maine," indicate the idealism once taught in the old rural academies,—and it is taught there still. City men will stop wistfully on the street, in the first week of September, to watch the boys and girls go trudging off to their first day of school; men who believe in nothing else at least believe in that! And school and college and university remain, as in the beginning, the first garden-ground and the last refuge of literature.

That "town-meeting" which John Adams thought Virginia might do well to adopt has likewise become a symbol of American idealism. Together with the training-day, it represented the rights and duties and privileges of free men; the machinery of self-government. It was democracy, rather than "representative" government, under its purest aspect. Sentiments of responsibility to the town, the political unit, and to the Commonwealth, the group of units, were bred there. Likewise, it was a training-school for sententious speech and weighty action; its roots, as historians love to demonstrate, run back very far; and though the modern drift to cities has made its machinery ineffective in the larger communities, it remains a perpetual spring or feeding stream to the broader currents of our national life. Without an understanding of the town-meeting and its equivalents, our political literature loses much of its significance. Like the school-house and meeting-house, it has become glorified by our men of letters. John Fiske and other historians have celebrated it in some of the most brilliant pages of our political writing; and that citizen literature, so deeply characteristic of us, found in the plain, forthright, and public-spirited tone of town-meeting discussions its keynote. The spectacular debates of our national history, the dramatic contests in the great arena of the Senate Chamber, the discussions before huge popular audiences in the West, have maintained the civic point of view, have developed and dignified and enriched the prose style first employed by American freemen in deciding their local affairs in the presence of their neighbors. "I am a part of this people," said Lincoln proudly in one of his famous debates of 1858; "I was raised just a little east of here"; and this nearness to the audience, this directness and simplicity and genuineness of our best political literature, its homely persuasiveness and force, is an inheritance of the town-meeting.

Bible and meeting-house, school-house and town-meeting, thus illustrate concretely the responsiveness of the American character to idealistic impulses. They are external symbols of a certain state of mind. It may indeed be urged that they are primarily signs of a moral and social or institutional trend, and are therefore non-literary evidence of American idealism. Nevertheless, institutional as they may be deemed, they lie close to that poetry of daily duty in which our literature has not been poor. They are fundamentally related to that attitude of mind, that habitual temper of the spirit, which has produced, in all countries of settled use and wont, the literature of idealism. Brunetière said of Flaubert's most famous woman character that poor Emma Bovary, the prey and the victim of Romantic desires, was after all much like the rest of us except that she lacked the intelligence to perceive the charm and poetry of the daily task. We have already touched upon the purely romantic side of American energy and of American imagination, and we must shortly look more closely still at those impulses of daring, those moods of heightened feeling, that intensified individualism, the quest of strangeness and terror and wild beauty, which characterize our romantic writing. But this romanticism is, as it were, a segment of the larger circle of idealism. It is idealism accentuated by certain factors, driven to self-expression by the passions of scorn or of desire; it exceeds, in one way or another, the normal range of experience and emotion. Our romantic American literature is doubtless our greatest. And yet some of the most characteristic tendencies of American writing are to be found in the poetry of daily experience, in the quiet accustomed light that falls upon one's own doorway and garden, in the immemorial charm of going forth to one's labor and returning in the evening,—poetry old as the world.

Let us see how this glow of idealism touches some of the more intimate aspects of human experience. "Out of the three Reverences," says Wilhelm Meister, "springs the highest Reverence, Reverence for Oneself." Open the pages of Hawthorne. Moving wholly within the framework of established institutions, with no desire to shatter the existing scheme of social order, choosing as its heroes men of themeeting-house, town-meeting, and training-day, how intensely nevertheless does the imagination of this fiction-writer illuminate the Body and the Soul!

Take first the Body. The inheritance of English Puritanism may be traced throughout our American writing, in its reverence for physical purity. The result is something unique in literary history. Continental critics, while recognizing the intellectual and artistic powers revealed in The Scarlet Letter, have seldom realized the awfulness, to the Puritan mind, of the very thought of an adulterous minister. That a priest in southern Europe should break his vows is indeed scandalous; but the sin is regarded as a failure of the natural man to keep a vow requiring supernatural grace for its fulfilment; it may be that the priest had no vocation for his sacred office; he is unfrocked, punished, forgotten, yet a certain mantle of human charity still covers his offence. But in the Puritan scheme (and The Scarlet Letter, save for that one treacherous, warm human moment in the woodland where "all was spoken," lies wholly within the set framework of Puritanism) there is no forgiveness for a sin of the flesh. There is only Law, Law stretching on into infinitude until the mind shudders at it. Hawthorne knew his Protestant New England through and through. The Scarlet Letter is the most striking example in our national literature of that idealization of physical purity, but hundreds of other romances and poems, less morbid if less great, assert in unmistakable terms the same moral conviction, the same ideal.

Yet, in spite of its theme, there was never a less adulterous novel than this book which plays so artistically with the letter A. The body is branded, is consumed, is at last, perhaps, transfigured by the intense rays of light emitted from the suffering soul.

"The soul is form and doth the body make."

In this intense preoccupation with the Soul, Hawthorne's romance is in unison with the more mystical and spiritual utterances of Catholicism as well as of Protestantism. It was in part a resultant of that early American isolation which contributed so effectively to the artistic setting of The Scarlet Letter. But in his doctrine of spiritual integrity, in the agonized utterance, "Be true—be true!" as well as inhis reverence for purity of the body, our greatest romancer was typical of the imaginative literature of his countrymen. The restless artistic experiments of Poe presented the human body in many a ghastly and terrifying aspect of illness and decay, and distorted by all passions save one. His imagination was singularly sexless.

Pathological students have pointed out the relation between this characteristic of Poe's writing, and his known tendencies toward opium-eating, alcoholism, and tuberculosis. But no such explanation is at hand to elucidate the absence of sexual passion from the novels of the masculine-minded Fenimore Cooper. One may say, indeed, that Cooper's novels, like Scott's, lack intensity of spiritual vision; that their tone is consonant with the views of a sound Church of England parson in the eighteenth century; and that the absence of physical passion, like the absence of purely spiritual insight, betrays a certain defect in Cooper's imaginative grasp and depth. But it is better criticism, after all, to remember that these three pioneers in American fiction-writing were composing for an audience in which Puritan traditions or tastes were predominant. Not one of the three men but would have instantly sacrificed an artistic effect, legitimate in the eyes of Fielding or Goethe or Balzac, rather than — in the phrase so often satirized — "bring a blush to the cheek of innocence." In other words, the presence of a specific audience, accustomed to certain Anglo-Saxon and Puritanic restraint of topic and of speech, has from the beginning of our imaginative literature coöperated with the instinct of our writers. That Victorian reticence which is so plainly seen even in such full-bodied writers as Dickens or Thackeray — a reticence which men like Mr. Bernard Shaw and Mr. Galsworthy and Mr. Wells think so hypocritical and dangerous to society and which they have certainly done their utmost to abolish — has hitherto dominated our American writing. The contemporary influence of great Continental writers to whom reticence is unknown, combined with the influence of a contemporary opera and drama to which reticence would be unprofitable, are now assaulting this dominant convention. Very possibly it is doomed. But it is only within recent years that its rule has been questioned.

One result of it may, I think, be fairly admitted. While very few writers of eminence, after all, in any country, wish to bring a "blush to the cheek of innocence," they naturally wish, as Thackeray put it in one of the best-known of his utterances, to be permitted to depict a man to the utmost of their power. American literary conventions, like English conventions, have now and again laid a restraining and compelling hand upon the legitimate exercise of this artistic instinct; and this fact has coöperated with many social, ethical, and perhaps physiological causes to produce a thinness or bloodlessness in our books. They are graceful, pleasing, but pale, like one of those cool whitish uncertain skies of an American spring. They lack "body," like certain wines. It is not often that we can produce a real Burgundy. We have had many distinguished fiction-writers, but none with the physical gusto of a Fielding, a Smollett, or even a Dickens, who, idealist and romanticist as he was, and Victorian as were his artistic preferences, has this animal life which tingles upon every page. We must confess that there is a certain quality of American idealism which is covertly suspicious or openly hostile to the glories of bodily sensation. Emerson's thin high shoulders peep up reproachfully above the desk; Lanier is playing his reproachful flute; Longfellow reads Frémont's Rocky Mountain experiences while lying abed, and sighs "But, ah, the discomforts!"; Irving's Astoria, superb as were the possibilities of its physical background, tastes like parlor exploration. Even Dana's Before the Mast and Parkman's Oregon Trail, transcripts of robust actual experience, and admirable books, reveal a sort of physical paleness compared with Turgenieff's Notes of a Sportsman and Tolstoï's Sketches of Sebastopol and the Crimea. They are Harvard undergraduate writing, after all!

These facts illustrate anew that standing temptation of the critic of American literature to palliate literary shortcomings by the plea that we possess certain admirable non-literary qualities. The dominant idealism of the nation has levied, or seemed to levy, a certain tax upon our writing. Some instincts, natural to the full-blooded utterance of Continental literature, have been starved or eliminated here. Very well. The characteristic American retort to this assertion would be: Better our long record and habit of idealism than a few masterpieces more or less. As a people, we have cheerfully accepted the Puritan restraint of speech, we have respected the shamefaced conventions of decent and social utterance. Like the men and women described in Locker-Lampson's verses, Americans "eat, and drink, and scheme, and plod, — They go to church on Sunday; And many are afraid of God — And more of Mrs. Grundy."

Now Mrs. Grundy is assuredly not the most desirable of literary divinities, but the student of classical literature can easily think of other divinities, celebrated in exquisite Greek and Roman verse, who are distinctly less desirable still.

"Not passion, but sentiment," said Hawthorne, in a familiar passage of criticism of his own Twice-Told Tales. How often must the student of American literature echo that half-melancholy but just verdict, as he surveys the transition from the spiritual intensity of a few of our earlier writers to the sentimental qualities which have brought popular recognition to the many. Take the word "soul" itself. Calvinism shadowed and darkened the meaning, perhaps, and yet its spiritual passion made the word "soul" sublime. The reaction against Calvinism has made religion more human, natural, and possibly more Christlike, but "soul" has lost the thrilling solemnity with which Edwards pronounced the word. Emerson and Hawthorne, far as they had escaped from the bonds of their ancestral religion, still utter the word "soul" with awe. But in the popular sermon and hymn and story of our day, — with their search after the sympathetic and the sentimental, after what is called in magazine slang "heart-interest," — the word has lost both its intellectual distinction and its literary magic. It will regain neither until it is pronounced once more with spiritual passion.

But in literature, as in other things, we must take what we can get. The great mass of our American writing is sentimental, because it has been produced by, and for, an excessively sentimental people. The poems in Stedman's carefully chosen Anthology, the prose and verse in the two volume Stedman-Hutchinson collection of American Literature, the Library of Southern Literature, and similar sectional anthologies, the school Readers and Speakers, — particularly in the half-century between 1830 and 1880, — our newspapers andmagazines, — particularly the so-called "yellow" newspapers and the illustrated magazines typified by Harper's Monthly, — are all fairly dripping with sentiment. American oratory is notoriously the most sentimental oratory of the civilized world. The Congressional Record still presents such specimens of sentiment — delivered or given leave to be printed, it is true, for "home consumption" rather than to affect the course of legislation — as are inexplicable to an Englishman or a Frenchman or an Italian.

Immigrants as we all are, and migratory as we have ever been, — so much so that one rarely meets an American who was born in the house built by his grandfather, — we cling with peculiar fondness to the sentiment of "Home." The best-known American poem, for decades, was Samuel Woodworth's "Old Oaken Bucket," the favorite popular song was Stephen Foster's "My Old Kentucky Home," the favorite play was Denman Thompson's "Old Homestead." Without that appealing word "mother" the American melodrama would be robbed of its fifth act. Without pictures of "the child" the illustrated magazines would go into bankruptcy. No country has witnessed such a production of periodicals and books for boys and girls: France and Germany imitate in vain The Youth's Companion and St. Nicholas, as they did the stories of "Oliver Optic" and Little Women and Little Lord Fauntleroy.

The sentimental attitude towards women and children, which is one of the most typical aspects of American idealism, is constantly illustrated in our short stories. Bret Harte, disciple of Dickens as he was, and Romantic as was his fashion of dressing up his miners and gamblers, was accurately faithful to the American feeling towards the "kid" and the "woman." "Tennessee's Partner," "The Luck of Roaring Camp," "Christmas at Sandy Bar," are obvious examples. Owen Wister's stories are equally faithful and admirable in this matter. The American girl still does astonishing things in international novels, as she has continued to do since the eighteen-sixties, but they are astonishing mainly to the European eye and against the conventionalized European background. She does the same things at home, and neither she nor her mother sees why she should not, so universal among us is the chivalrous interpretation of actions and situations which amaze the European observer. The popular American literature which recognizes and encourages this position of the "young girl" in our social structure is a literature primarily of sentiment. The note of passion—in the European sense of that word—jars and shatters it. The imported "problem-play," written for an adult public in Paris or London, introduces social facts and intellectual elements almost wholly alien to the experience of American matinée audiences. Disillusioned historians of our literature have instanced this unsophistication as a proof of our national inexperience; yet it is often a sort of radiant and triumphant unsophistication which does not lose its innocence in parting with its ignorance.

That sentimental idealization of classes, whether peasant, bourgeois, or aristocratic, which has long been a feature of Continental and English poetry and fiction, is practically absent from American literature. Whatever the future may bring, there have hitherto been no fixed classes in American society. Webster was guilty of no exaggeration when he declared that the whole North was made up of laborers, and Lincoln spoke in the same terms in his well-known sentences about "hired laborers": "twenty-five years ago I was a hired laborer." The relative uniformity of economic and social conditions, which prevailed until toward the close of the nineteenth century, made, no doubt, for the happiness of the greatest number, but it failed, naturally, to afford that picturesqueness of class contrast and to stimulate that sentiment of class distinction, in which European literature is so rich.

Very interesting, in the light of contemporary economic conditions, is the effort made by American poets in the middle of the last century to glorify labor. They were not so much idealizing a particular laboring class, as endeavoring, in Whitman's words, "To teach the average man the glory of his walk and trade." Whitman himself sketched the American workman in almost every attitude which appealed to his own sense of the picturesque and heroic. But years before Leaves of Grass was published, Whittier had celebrated in his Songs of Labor the glorified images of lumberman and drover, shoemaker and fisherman. Lucy Larcom and the authors of The Lowell Offeringportrayed the fine idealism of the young women—of the best American stock—who went enthusiastically to work in the cotton-mills of Lowell and Lawrence, or who bound shoes by their own firesides on the Essex County farms. That glow of enthusiasm for labor was chiefly moral, but it was poetical as well. The changes which have come over the economic and social life of America are nowhere more sharply indicated than in that very valley of the Merrimac where, sixty and seventy years ago, one could "hear America singing." There are few who are singing to-day in the cotton-mills; the operators, instead of girls from the hill-farms, are Greeks, Lithuanians, Armenians, Italians. Whittier's drovers have gone forever; the lumbermen and deep-sea fishermen have grown fewer, and the men who still swing the axes and haul the frozen cod-lines are mostly aliens. The pride that once broke into singing has turned harsh and silent. "Labor" looms vast upon the future political and social horizon, but the songs of labor have lost the lyric note. They have turned into the dramas and tragedies of labor, as portrayed with the swift and fierce insistence of the short story, illustrated by the Kodak. In the great agricultural sections of the West and South the old bucolic sentiment still survives,—that simple joy of seeing the "frost upon the pumpkin" and "the fodder in the stock" which Mr. James Whitcomb Riley has sung with such charming fidelity to the type. But even on the Western farms toil has grown less manual. It is more a matter of expert handling of machinery. Reaping and binding may still have their poet, but he needs to be a Kipling rather than a Burns.

Our literature, then, reveals few traces of idealization of a class, and but little idealization of trades or callings. Neither class nor calling presents anything permanent to the American imagination, or stands for anything ultimate in American experience. On the other hand, our writing is rich in local sentiment and sectional loyalty. The short story, which has seized so greedily the more dramatic aspects of American energy, has been equally true to the quiet background of rural scenery and familiar ways. American idealism, as shown in the transformation of the lesser loyalties of home and countryside into the larger loyalties of state and section, and the absorption of these, in turn, into the emotions of nationalism, is particularly illustrated in our political verse. A striking example of the imaginative visualization of the political units of a state is the spirited roll-call of the counties in Whittier's "Massachusetts to Virginia." But the burden of that fine poem, after all, is the essential unity of Massachusetts as a sovereign state, girding herself to repel the attack of another sovereign state, Virginia. Now the evolution of our political history, both local and national, has tended steadily, for half a century, to the obliteration, for purposes of the imagination, of county lines within state lines. At the last Republican state convention held in Massachusetts, there were no county banners displayed, for the first time in half a century. Many a city-dweller to-day cannot tell in what county he is living unless he has happened to make a transfer of real estate. State lines themselves are fading away. The federal idea has triumphed. Doubtless the majority of the fellow citizens of John Randolph of Roanoke were all the more proud of him because the poet could say of him, in writing an admiring and mournful epitaph: —

"Beyond Virginia's border lineHis patriotism perished."

The great collections of Civil War verse, which are lying almost unread in the libraries, are store-houses of this ancient state pride and jealousy, which was absorbed so fatally into the larger sectional antagonism. "Maryland, my Maryland" gave place to "Dixie," just as Whittier's "Massachusetts to Virginia" was forgotten when marching men began to sing "John Brown's Body" and "The Battle Hymn of the Republic." The literature of sectionalism still lingers in its more lovable aspect in the verse and fiction which still celebrates the fairer side of the civilization of the Old South: its ideals of chivalry and local loyalty, its gracious women and gallant men. Our literature needs to cultivate this provincial affection for the past, as an offset to the barren uniformity which the federal scheme allows. But the ultimate imaginative victory, like the actual political victory of the Civil War, is with the thought and feeling of Nationalism. It is foreshadowed in that passionate lyric cry of Lowell, which sums up so much and, like all true passion, anticipates so much: —

"O Beautiful! my Country!"

The literary record of American idealism thus illustrates how deeply the conception of Nationalism has affected the imagination of our countrymen. The literary record of the American conception of liberty runs further back. Some historians have allowed themselves to think that the American notion of liberty is essentially declamatory, a sort of futile echo of Patrick Henry's "Give me Liberty or give me Death"; and not only declamatory, but hopelessly theoretical and abstract. They grant that it was a trumpet-note, no doubt, for agitators against the Stamp Act, and for pamphleteers like Thomas Paine; that it may have been a torch for lighting dark and weary ways in the Revolutionary War; but they believe it likewise to be a torch which gleams with the fire caught from France and which was passed back to France in turn when her own great bonfire was ready for lighting. The facts, however, are inconsistent with this picturesque theory of contemporary reactionists. It is true that the word "liberty" has been full of temptation for generations of American orators, that it has become an idol of the forum, and often a source of heat rather than of light. But to treat American Liberty as if she habitually wore the red cap is to nourish a Francophobia as absurd as Edmund Burke's. The sober truth is that the American working theory of Liberty is singularly like St. Paul's. "Ye have been called unto liberty; only use not liberty for an occasion to the flesh." A few sentences from John Winthrop, written in 1645, are significant: "There is a twofold liberty, natural ... and civil or federal. The first is common to man with beasts and other creatures. By this, man, as he stands in relation to man simply, hath liberty to do what he lists; it is a liberty to evil as well as to good. This liberty is incompatible and inconsistent with authority.... The other kind of liberty I call civil or federal, it may also be termed moral.... This liberty is the proper end and object of authority, and cannot subsist without it; and it is a liberty to that only which is good, just, and honest. This liberty you are to stand for, with the hazard (not only of your goods, but) of your lives, if need be.... This liberty is maintained and exercised in a way of subjection to authority; it is of the same kind of liberty wherewith Christ hath made us free."

There speaks the governor, the man of affairs, the typical citizen of the future republic. The liberty to do as one pleases is a dream of the Renaissance; but out of dreamland it does not work. Nobody, even in revolutionary France, imagines that it will work. Jefferson, who is popularly supposed to derive his notion of liberty from French theorists, is to all practical purposes nearer to John Winthrop than he is to Rousseau.

The splendid phrases of his "Declaration" are sometimes characterized as abstractions. They are really generalizations from past political experience. An arbitrary king, assuming a liberty to do as he liked, had encroached upon the long-standing customs and authority of the colonists. Jefferson, at the bidding of the Continental Congress, served notice of the royal trespass, and incidentally produced (as Lincoln said) a "standard maxim for free society."

It is true, no doubt, that the word "liberty" became in Jefferson's day, and later, a mere partisan or national shibboleth, standing for no reality, degraded to a catchword, a symbol of antagonism to Great Britain. In the political debates and the impressive prose and verse of the anti-slavery struggle, the word became once more charged with vital meaning; it glowed under the heat and pressure of an idea. Towards the end of the nineteenth century it went temporarily out of fashion. The late Colonel Higginson, an ideal type of what Europeans call an "1848" man, attended at the close of the century some sessions of the American Historical Association. In his own address, at the closing dinner, he remarked that there was one word for which he had listened in vain during the reading of the papers by the younger men. It was the word "liberty." One of the younger school retorted promptly that since we had the thing liberty, we had no need to glorify the word. But Colonel Higginson, stanch adherent as he was of the "good old cause," was not convinced. Like many another lover of American letters, he thought that William Vaughn Moody's "Ode in Time of Hesitation" deserved a place by the side of Lowell's "Commemoration Ode," and that when the ultimate day of reckoning comes for the whole muddled Imperialistic business, the standard of reckoning must be "liberty" as Winthrop and Jefferson and Lincoln and Lowell and Vaughn Moody understood the word.

In the mean time we must confess that the history of our literature, with a few noble exceptions, shows a surprising defect in the passion for freedom. Tennyson's famous lines about "Freedom broadening slowly down from precedent to precedent" are perfectly American in their conservative tone; while it is Englishmen like Byron and Landor and Shelley and Swinburne who have written the most magnificent republican poetry. The "land of the free" turns to the monarchic mother country, after all, for the glow and thunder and splendor of the poetry of freedom. It is one of the most curious phenomena in the history of literature. Shall we enter the preoccupation plea once more? Enjoying the thing liberty, have we been therefore less concerned with the idea? Or is it simply another illustration of the defective passion of American literature?

Yet there is one phase of political loyalty which has been cherished by the imagination of Americans, and which has inspired noteworthy oratory and noble political prose. It is the sentiment of Union. In one sense, of course, this dates back to the period of Franklin's bon motabout our all hanging together, or hanging separately. It is found in Hamilton's pamphlets, in Paine's Crisis, in the Federalist, in Washington's "Farewell Address." It is peculiarly associated with the name and fame of Daniel Webster, and, to a less degree, with the career of Henry Clay. In the stress of the debate over slavery, many a Northerner with abolitionist convictions, like the majority of Southerners with slave-holding convictions, forgot the splendid peroration of Webster's "Reply to Hayne" and were willing to "let the Union go." But in the four tragic and heroic years that followed the firing upon the American flag at Fort Sumter the sentiment of Union was made sacred by such sacrifices as the patriotic imagination of a Clay or a Webster had never dreamed. A new literature resulted. A lofty ideal of indissoluble Union was preached in pulpits, pleaded for in editorials, sung in lyrics, and woven into the web of fiction. Edward Everett Hale's Man Without a Country became one of the most poignantly moving of American stories. In Walt Whitman'sDrum-Taps and his later poems, the "Union of these States" became transfigured with mystical significance: no longer a mere political compact, dissoluble at will, but a spiritual entity, a new incarnation of the soul of man.

We must deal later with that American instinct of fellowship which Whitman believed to have been finally cemented by the Civil War, and which has such import for the future of our democracy. There are likewise communal loyalties, glowing with the new idealism which has come with the twentieth century: ethical, municipal, industrial, and artistic movements which are full of promise for the higher life of the country, but which have not yet had time to express themselves adequately in literature. There are stirrings of racial loyalty among this and that element of our composite population,—as for instance among the gifted younger generation of American Jews,—a racial loyalty not antagonistic to the American current of ideas, but rather in full unison with it. Internationalism itself furnishes motives for the activity of the noblest imaginations, and the true literature of internationalism has hardly yet begun. It is in the play and counterplay of these new forces that the American literature of the twentieth century must measure itself. Communal feelings novel to Americans bred under the accepted individualism will doubtless assert themselves in our prose and verse. But it is to be remembered that the best writing thus far produced on American soil has been a result of the old conditions: of the old "Reverences"; of the pioneer training of mind and body; of the slow tempering of the American spirit into an obstinate idealism. We do not know what course the ship may take in the future, but

"We know what Master laid thy keel,What Workman wrought thy ribs of steel,Who made each mast and sail and rope,What anvil rang, what hammers beat,In what a forge and what a heatWere shaped the anchors of thy hope!"

IV

Romance and Reaction

The characteristic attitude of the American mind, as we have seen, is one of idealism. We may now venture to draw a smaller circle within that larger circle of idealistic impulses, and to label the smaller circle "romance." Here, too, as with the word "idealism," although we are to make abundant use of literary illustrations of national tendencies, we have no need of a severely technical definition of terms. When we say, "Tom is an idealist" and "Lorenzo is a romantic fellow," we convey at least one tolerably clear distinction between Tom and Lorenzo. The idealist has a certain characteristic habit of mind or inclination of spirit. When confronted by experience, he reacts in a certain way. In his individual and social impulses, in the travail of his soul, or in his commerce with his neighbors and the world, he behaves in a more or less well-defined fashion. The romanticist, when confronted by the same objects and experiences, exhibits another type of behavior. Lorenzo, though he be Tom's brother, is a different fellow; he is — in the opinion of his friends, at least — a rather more peculiar person, a creature of more varying moods, of heightened feelings, of stranger ways. Like Tom, he is a person of sentiment, but his sentiment attaches itself, not so much to everyday aspects of experience, as to that which is unusual or terrifying, lovely or far away; he possesses, or would like to possess, bodily or spiritual daring. He has the adventurous heart. He is of those who love to go down to the sea in ships and do business in great waters. Lorenzo the romanticist is made of no finer clay than Tom the idealist, but his nerves are differently tuned. Your deep-sea fisherman, after all, is only a fisherman at bottom. That is to say, he too is an idealist, but he wants to catch different species of fish from those which drop into the basket of the landsman. Precisely what he covets, perhaps he does not know. I was once foolish enough to ask an old Alsatian soldier who was patiently holding his rod over a most unpromising canal near Strassburg, what kind of fish he was fishing for. "All kinds," was his rebuking answer, and I took off my hat to the veteran romanticist.

The words "romance" and "romanticism" have been repeated to the ears of our generation with wearisome iteration. Not the least of the good luck of Wordsworth and Coleridge lay in the fact that they scarcely knew that they were "romanticists." Middle-aged readers of the present day may congratulate themselves that in their youth they read Wordsworth and Coleridge simply because it was Wordsworth and Coleridge and not documents illustrating the history of the romantic movement. But the rising generation is sophisticated. For better or worse it has been taught to distinguish between the word "romance" on the one side, and the word "romanticism" on the other. "Romantic" is a useful but overworked adjective which attaches itself indiscriminately to both "romance" and "romanticism." Professor Vaughan, for example, and a hundred other writers, have pointed out that in the narrower and more usual sense, the words "romance" and "romanticism" point to a love of vivid coloring and strongly marked contrasts; to a craving for the unfamiliar, the marvellous, and the supernatural. In the wider and less definite sense, they signify a revolt from the purely intellectual view of man's nature; a recognition of the instincts and the passions, a vague intimation of sympathy between man and the world around him,—in one word, the sense of mystery. The narrower and the broader meanings pass into one another by imperceptible shades. They are affected by the well-known historic conditions for romantic feeling in the different European countries. The common factor, of course, is the man with the romantic world set in his heart. It is Gautier with his love of color, Victor Hugo enraptured with the sound of words, Heine with his self-destroying romantic irony, Novalis with his blue flower, and Maeterlinck with his Blue Bird.

But these romantic men of letters, writing in epochs of romanticism, are by no means the only children of romance. Sir Humphrey Gilbert and Sir Walter Raleigh were as truly followers of "the gleam" as were Spenser or Marlowe. The spirit of romance is found wherever and whenever men say to themselves, as Don Quixote's niece said of her uncle, that "they wish better bread than is made of wheat," or when they look within their own hearts, and assert, as the poet Young said in 1759, long before the English romantic movement had begun, "there is more in the spirit of man than mere prose-reason can fathom."

We are familiar, perhaps too remorsefully familiar, with the fact that romance is likely to run a certain course in the individual and then to disappear. Looking back upon it afterward, it resembles the upward and downward zigzag of a fever chart. It has in fact often been described as a measles, a disease of which no one can be particularly proud, although he may have no reason to blush for it. Southey said that he was no more ashamed of having been a republican than of having been a boy. Well, people catch Byronism, and get over it, much as Southey got over his republicanism. In fact Byron himself lived long enough—though he died at thirty-six—to outgrow his purely "Byronic" phase, and to smile at it as knowingly as we do. Coleridge's blossoming period as a romantic poet was tragically brief. Keats and Shelley had the good fortune to die in the fulness of their romantic glory. They did not outlive their own poetic sense of the wonder and mystery of the world. Yet many an old poet like Tennyson and Browning has preserved his romance to the end. Tennyson dies at eighty-three with the full moonlight streaming through the oriel window upon his bed, and with his fingers clasping Shakespeare'sCymbeline.

With most of us commonplace persons, however, a reaction from the romantic is almost inevitable. The romantic temperament cannot long keep the pitch. Poe could indeed do it, although he hovered at times near the border of insanity. Hawthorne went for relief to his profane sea-captains and the carnal-minded superannuated employees of the Salem Custom House. "The weary weight of all this unintelligible world" presses too hard on most of those who stop to think about it. The simplest way of relief is to shrug one's shoulders and let the weight go. That is to say, we cease being poets, we are no longer the children of romance, although we may remain idealists. Perhaps it is external events that change, rather than we ourselves. The restoration of the Bourbons, the Revolutions of 1830 and 1848, make and unmake romantics. Often society catches up with the romanticist; he is no longer a soldier of revolt; he has become a "respectable." Or, while remaining a poet, he shifts his attention to some more familiar segment of the idealistic circle. He sings about his wife instead of the wife of somebody else. Like Wordsworth, he takes for his theme a Mary Hutchinson instead of the unknown and hauntingly alluring figure of Lucy. To put it differently, the high light, the mysterious color of dawn or sunset disappears from his picture of human life. Or, the high light may be diffused in a more tranquil radiance over the whole surface of experience. Such an artist may remain a true painter or poet, but he is not a romantic poet or painter any longer. He has, like the aging Emerson, taken in sail; the god Terminus has said to him, "no more."

One must of course admit that the typical romanticist has often been characterized by certain intellectual and moral weaknesses. But the great romance men, like Edmund Spenser, for example, may not possess these weaknesses at all. Robert Louis Stevenson was passionately in love with the romantic in life and with romanticism in literature; but it did not make him eccentric, weak, or empty. His instinct for enduring romance was so admirably fine that it brought strength to the sinews of his mind, light and air and fire to his soul. Among the writers of our own day, it is Mr. Kipling who has written some of the keenest satire upon romantic foibles, while never ceasing to salute his real mistress, the true romance.

"Who wast, or yet the Lights were set,A whisper in the void,Who shalt be sung through planets youngWhen this is clean destroyed."

What are the causes of American romance, the circumstances and qualities that have produced the romantic element in American life and character? Precisely as with the individual artist or man of letters, we touch first of all upon certain temperamental inclinations. It is a question again of the national mind, of the differentiation of the race under new climatic and physical conditions. We have to reckon with the headiness and excitability of youth. It was young men who emigrated hither, just as in the eighteen-sixties it was young men who filled the Northern and the Southern armies. The first generations of American immigration were made up chiefly of vigorous, imaginative, and daring youth. The incapables came later. It is, I think, safe to assert that the colonists of English stock, even as late as 1790,—when more than ninety per cent of the population of America had in their veins the blood of the British Isles,—were more responsive to romantic impulses than their English cousins. For that matter, an Irishman or a Welshman is more romantic than an Englishman to-day.

From the very beginning of the American settlements, likewise, there were evidences of the weaker, the over-excitable side of the romantic temper. There were volatile men like Morton of Merrymount; there were queer women like Anne Hutchinson, admirable woman as she was; among the wives of the colonists there were plenty of Emily Dickinsons in the germ. Among the men, there were schemes that came to nothing. There were prototypes of Colonel Sellers; a temperamental tendency toward that recklessness and extravagance which later historical conditions stimulated and confirmed. The more completely one studies the history of our forefathers on American soil, the more deeply does one become conscious of the prevailing atmosphere of emotionalism.

Furthermore, as one examines the historic conditions under which the spirit of American romance has been preserved and heightened from time to time, one becomes aware that although ours is rather a romance of wonder than of beauty, the spirit of beauty is also to be found. The first fervors of the romance of discovery were childlike in their eagerness. Hakluyt's Voyages, John Smith's True Relation of Virginia, Thomas Morton's New England's Canaan, all appeal to the sense of the marvellous.

Listen to Morton's description of Cape Ann. I can never read it without thinking of Botticelli's picture of Spring, so naïvely does this picturesque rascal suffuse his landscape with the feeling for beauty:—

"In the Moneth of June, Anno Salutis 1622, it was my chaunce to arrive in the parts of New England with 30. Servants, and provision of all sorts fit for a plantation: and whiles our howses were building, I did indeavour to take a survey of the Country: The more I looked, the more I liked it. And when I had more seriously considered of the bewty of the place, with all her faire indowments, I did not think that in all the knowne world it could be paralel'd, for so many goodly groves of trees, dainty fine round rising hillucks, delicate faire large plaines, sweete cristall fountaines, and cleare running streames that twine in fine meanders through the meads, making so sweete a murmering noise to heare as would even lull the sences with delight a sleepe, so pleasantly doe they glide upon the pebble stones, jetting most jocundly where they doe meete and hand in hand runne downe to Neptunes Court, to pay the yearely tribute which they owe to him as soveraigne Lord of all the springs. Contained within the volume of the Land, Fowles in abundance, Fish in multitude; and discovered, besides, Millions of Turtledoves on the greene boughes, which sate pecking of the full ripe pleasant grapes that were supported by the lusty trees, whose fruitful loade did cause the armes to bend: while here and there dispersed, you might see Lillies and the Daphnean-tree: which made the Land to mee seeme paradice: for in mine eie t'was Natures Masterpeece; Her cheifest Magazine of all where lives her store: if this Land be not rich, then is the whole world poore."

This is the Morton who, a few years later, settled at Merrymount. Let me condense the story of his settlement, from the narrative of the stout-hearted Governor William Bradford's History of Plymouth Plantation: —

"And Morton became lord of misrule, and maintained (as it were) a schoole of Athisme. And after they had gott some good into their hands, and gott much by trading with the Indeans, they spent it as vainly, in quaffing & drinking both wine & strong waters in great exsess, and, as some reported 10£. worth in a morning. They allso set up a May-pole, drinking and dancing aboute it many days togeather, inviting the Indean women, for their consorts, dancing and frisking togither, (like so many fairies, or furies rather,) and worse practises. As if they had anew revived & celebrated the feasts of the Roman Goddes Flora, or the beasly practieses of the madd Bacchinalians. Morton likewise (to shew his poetrie) composed sundry rimes & verses, some tending to lasciviousnes, and others to the detraction & scandall of some persons, which he affixed to this idle or idoll May-polle. They chainged allso the name of their place, and in stead of calling it Mounte Wollaston, they call it Merie-mounte, as if this joylity would have lasted ever."

But it did not last long. Bradford and other leaders of the plantations "agreed by mutual consent" to "suppress Morton and his consorts." "In a friendly and neighborly way" they admonished him. "Insolently he persisted." "Upon which they saw there was no way but to take him by force." "So they mutually resolved to proceed," and sent Captain Standish to summon him to yield. But, says Bradford, Morton and some of his crew came out, not to yield, but to shoot; all of them rather drunk; Morton himself, with a carbine almost half filled with powder and shot, had thought to have shot Captain Standish, "but he stepped to him and put by his piece and took him."

It is not too fanciful to say that with those stern words of Governor Bradford the English Renaissance came to an end. The dream of a lawless liberty which has been dreamed and dreamed out so many times in the history of the world was over, for many a day. It was only a hundred years earlier that Rabelais had written over the doors of his ideal abbey, the motto "Do what thou wilt." It is true that Rabelais proposed to admit to his Abbey of Thélème only such men and women as were virtuously inclined. We do not know how many persons would have been able and willing to go into residence there. At any rate, two hundred years went by in New England after the fall of Morton before any notable spirit dared to cherish once more the old Renaissance ideal. At last, in Emerson's doctrine that all things are lawful because Nature is good and human nature is divine, we have a curious parallel to the doctrine of Rabelais. It was the old romance of human will under a new form and voiced in new accents. Yet in due time the hard facts of human nature reasserted themselves and put this romantic transcendentalism by, even as the implacable Myles Standish put by that heavily loaded fowling-piece of the drunken Morton.

But men believed in miracles in the first century of colonization, and they will continue at intervals to believe in them until human nature is no more. The marvellous happenings recorded in Cotton Mather's Magnalia no longer excite us to any "suspension of disbelief." We doubt the story of Pocahontas. The fresh romantic enthusiasm of a settler like Crèvecœur seems curiously juvenile to-day, as does the romantic curiosity of Chateaubriand concerning the Mississippi and the Choctaws, or the zeal of Wordsworth and Coleridge over their dream of a "panti-Socratic" community in the unknown valley of the musically-sounding Susquehanna. Inexperience is a perpetual feeder of the springs of romance. John Wesley, it will be remembered, went out to the colony of Georgia full of enthusiasm for converting the Indians; but as he naïvely remarks in his Journal, he "neither found or heard of any Indians on the continent of America, who had the least desire of being instructed." The sense of fact, in other words, supervenes, and the glory disappears from the face of romance. The humor of Mark Twain's Innocents Abroad turns largely upon this sense of remorseless fact confronting romantic inexperience.

American history, however, has been marked by certain great romantic passions that seem endowed with indestructible vitality. The romance of discovery, the fascination of the forest and sea, the sense of danger and mystery once aroused by the very word "redskin," have all moulded and will continue to mould the national imagination. How completely the romance of discovery may be fused with the glow of humanitarian and religious enthusiasm has been shown once for all in the brilliant pages of Parkman's story of the Jesuit missions in Canada. Pictorial romance can scarcely go further than this. In the crisis of Chateaubriand's picturesque and passionate tale of the American wilderness, no one can escape the thrilling, haunting sound of the bell from the Jesuit chapel, as it tolls in the night and storm that were fatal to the happiness of Atala. One scarcely need say that the romance of missions has never faded from the American mind. I have known a sober New England deacon aged eighty-five, who disliked to die because he thought he should miss the monthly excitement of reading the Missionary Herald. The deacon's eyes, like the eyes of many an old sea-captain in Salem or Newburyport, were literally upon the ends of the earth. No one can reckon how many starved souls, deprived of normal outlet for human feeling, have found in this passionate curiosity and concern for the souls of black and yellow men and women in the antipodes, a constant source of beneficent excitement.

Nor is there any diminution of interest in the mere romance of adventure, in the stories of hunter and trapper, the journals of Lewis and Clarke, the narratives of Boone and Crockett. In writing his superb romances of the

Northern Lakes, the prairie and the sea, Fenimore Cooper had merely to bring to an artistic focus sentiments that lay deep in the souls of the great mass of his American readers. Students of our social life have pointed out again and again how deeply our national temperament has been affected by the existence, during nearly three hundred years, of an alien aboriginal race forever lurking upon the borders of our civilization. "Playing Indian" has been immensely significant, not merely in stimulating the outdoor activity of generations of American boys, but in teaching them the perennial importance of certain pioneer qualities of observation, resourcefulness, courage, and endurance which date from the time when the Indians were a daily and nightly menace. Even when the Indian has been succeeded by the cowboy, the spirit of romance still lingers, — as any collection of cowboy ballads will abundantly prove. And when the cowboys pass, and the real-estate dealers take possession of the field, one is tempted to say that romance flourishes more than ever.

In short, things are what we make them at the moment, what we believe them to be. In my grandfather's youth the West was in the neighborhood of Port Byron, New York, and when he journeyed thither from Massachusetts in the eighteen-twenties, the glory of adventure enfolded him as completely as the boys of the preceding generation had been glorified in the War of the Revolution, or the boys of the next generation when they went gold-seeking in California in 1849. The West, in short, means simply the retreating horizon, the beckoning finger of opportunity. Like Boston, it has been not a place, but a "state of mind."

"We must go, go, go away from here,On the other side the world we're overdue."

That is the song which sings itself forever in the heart of youth. Champlain and Cartier heard it in the sixteenth century, Bradford no less than Morton in the seventeenth. Some Eldorado has always been calling to the more adventurous spirits upon American soil. The passion of the forty-niner neither began nor ended with the discovery of gold in California. It is within us. It transmutes the harsh or drab-colored everyday routine into tissue of fairyland. It makes our "winning of the West" a magnificent national epic. It changes to-day the black belt of Texas, or the wheat-fields of Dakota, into pots of gold that lie at the end of rainbows, only that the pot of gold is actually there. The human hunger of it all, the gorgeous dream-like quality of it all, the boundlessness of the vast American spaces, the sense of forest and prairie and sky, are all inexplicably blended with our notion of the ideal America. Henry James once tried to explain the difference between Turgenieff and a typical French novelist by saying that the back door of the Russian's imagination was always open upon the endless Russian steppe. No one can understand the spirit of American romance if he is not conscious of this ever-present hinterland in which our spirits have, from the beginning, taken refuge and found solace.

We have already noticed, in the chapter on idealism, how swiftly the American imagination modifies the prosaic facts of everydayexperience. The idealistic glamour which falls upon the day's work changes easily, in the more emotional temperaments, and at times, indeed, in all of us, into the fervor of true romance. Then, the prosaic buying and selling becomes the "game." A combination of buyers and sellers becomes the "system." The place where these buyers and sellers most do congregate and concentrate becomes "Wall Street"—a sort of anthropomorphic monster which seems to buy and sell the bodies and souls of men. Seen half a continent away, through the mists of ignorance and prejudice and partisan passion, "Wall Street" has loomed like some vast Gibraltar. To the broker's clerk who earns his weekly salary in that street, the Nebraska notion of "Wall Street" is too grotesque for discussion.

How easily every phase of American business life may take on the hues of romance is illustrated by the history of our railroads. No wonder that Bret Harte wrote a poem about the meeting of the eastward and westward facing engines when the two sections of the Union Pacific Railroad at last drew near each other on the interminable plains and the two engines could talk. Of course what they said was poetry. There was a time when even the Erie Canal was poetic. The Panama Canal to-day, in the eyes of most Americans, is something other than a mere feat of engineering. We are doing more than making "the dirt fly." The canal represents victory over hostile forces, conquest of unwilling Nature, achievement of what had long been deemed impossible, the making not of a ditch, but of History.

So with all that American zest for camping, fishing, sailing, racing, which lies deep in the Anglo-Saxon, and which succeeds to the more primitive era of actual struggle against savage beasts or treacherous men or mysterious forests. It is at once an outlet and a nursery for romantic emotion. The out-of-doors movement which began with Thoreau's hut on Walden Pond, and which has gone on broadening and deepening to this hour, implies far more than mere variation from routine. It furnishes, indeed, a healthful escape from the terrific pressure of modern social and commercial exigencies. Yet its more important function is to provide for grown-ups a chance to "play Indian" too.

But outdoors and indoors, after all, lie in the heart and mind, rather than in the realm of actual experience. The romantic imagination insists upon taking its holiday, whether the man who possesses it gets his holiday or not. I have never known a more truly romantic figure than a certain tin-pedler in Connecticut who, in response to the question, "Do you do a good business?" made this perfectly Stevensonian reply: "Well, I make a living selling crockery and tinware, but my business is the propagation of truth."

This wandering idealist may serve to remind us again of the difference between romance and romanticism. The true romance is of the spirit. Romanticism shifts and changes with external fortunes, with altering emotions, with the alternate play of light and shade over the vast landscape of human experience. The typical romanticist, as we have seen, is a man of moods. It is only a Poe who can keep the pitch through the whole concert of experience. But the deeper romance of the spirit is oblivious of these changes of external fortune, this rising or falling of the emotional temperature. The moral life of America furnishes striking illustrations of the steadfastness with which certain moral causes have been kept, as it were, in the focus of intense feeling. Poetry, undefeated and unwavering poetry, has transfigured such practical propaganda as the abolition of slavery, the emancipation of woman, the fight against the liquor traffic, the emancipation of the individual from the clutches of economic and commercial despotism. Men like Colonel Thomas Wentworth Higginson, women like Julia Ward Howe, fought for these causes throughout their lives. Colonel Higginson's attitude towards women was not merely chivalric (for one may be chivalrous without any marked predisposition to romance), but nobly romantic also. James Russell Lowell, poet as he was, outlived that particular phase of romantic moral reform which he had been taught by Maria White. But in other men and women bred in that old New England of the eighteen-forties, the moral fervor knew no restraint. Garrison, although in many respects a most unromantic personality, was engaged in a task which gave him all the inspiration of romance. A romantic "atmosphere," fully as highly colored as any of the romantic atmospheres that we are accustomed to mark in literature, surrounded as with a luminous mist the figures of the New England transcendentalists. They, too, as Heine said of himself, were soldiers. They felt themselves enlisted for a long but ultimately victorious campaign. They were willing to pardon, in their comrades and in themselves, those imaginative excesses which resemble the physical excesses of a soldier's camp. Transcendentalism was thus a militant philosophy and religion, with both a destructively critical and a positively constructive creed. Channing, Parker, Alcott, Margaret Fuller, were warrior-priests, poets and prophets of a gallant campaign against inherited darkness and bigotry, and for the light.

The atmosphere of that score of years in New England was now superheated, now rarefied, thin, and cold; but it was never quite the normal atmosphere of every day. On the purely literary side, it is needless to say, these men and women sought inspiration in Coleridge and Carlyle and other English and German romanticists. In fact, the most enduring literature of New England between 1830 and 1865 was distinctly a romantic literature. It was rooted, however, not so much in those swift changes of historic condition, those startling liberations of the human spirit which gave inspiration to the romanticism of the Continent, as it was in the deep and vital fervor with which these New Englanders envisaged the problems of the moral life.

Other illustrations of the American capacity for romance lie equally close at hand. Take, for instance, the stout volume in which Mr. Burton Stevenson has collected the Poems of American History. Here are nearly seven hundred pages of closely printed patriotic verse. While Stedman's Anthology reveals no doubt national aspirations and national sentiment, as well as the emotional fervor of individuals, Mr. Stevenson's collection has the advantage of focussing this national feeling upon specific events. Stedman's Anthology is an enduring document of American idealism, touching in the sincerity of its poetic moods, pathetic in its long lists of men and women who are known by one poem only, or who have never, for one reason or another, fulfilled their poetic promise. The thousand poems which it contains are more striking, in fact, for their promise than for their performance. They are intimations of what American men and women would have liked to do or to be. In this sense, it is a precious volume, but it is certainly not commensurate, either in passion or in artistic perfection, with the forces of that American life which it tries to interpret. Indeed, Mr. Stedman, after finishing his task of compilation, remarked to more than one of his friends that what this country needed was some "adult male verse."

The Poems of American History collected by Mr. Stevenson are at least vigorous and concrete. One aspect of our history which especially lends itself to Mr. Stevenson's purpose is the romance which attaches itself to war. It is scarcely necessary to say nowadays that all wars, even the noblest, have had their sordid, grimy, selfish, bestial aspect; and that the intelligence and conscience of our modern world are more and more engaged in the task of making future wars impossible. But the slightest acquaintance with American history reveals the immense reservoir of romantic emotion which has been drawn upon in our national struggles. War, of course, is an immemorial source of romantic feeling. William James's notable essay on "A Moral Substitute for War" endeavored to prove that our modern economic and social life, if properly organized, would give abundant outlet and satisfaction to those romantic impulses which formerly found their sole gratification in battle. Many of us believe that he was right; but for the moment we must look backward and not forward.

We must remember the stern if rude poetry inspired by our Revolutionary struggle, the romantic halo that falls upon the youthful figure of Nathan Hale, the baleful light that touches the pale face of Benedict Arnold, the romance of the Bennington fight to the followers of Stark and Ethan Allen, the serene voice of the "little captain," John Paul Jones: — "We have not struck, we have just begun our part of the fighting." The colors of romance still drape the Chesapeake and the Shannon, Tecumseh and Tippecanoe. The hunters of Kentucky, the explorers of the Yellowstone and the Columbia, the emigrants who left their bones along the old Santa Fé Trail, are our Homeric men.

The Mexican War affords pertinent illustration, not only of romance, but of reaction. The earlier phases of the Texan struggle for independence have much of the daring, the splendid rashness, the glorious and tragic catastrophes of the great romantic adventures of the Old World. It is not the Texans only who still "remember the Alamo," but when those brilliant and dramatic adventures of border warfare became drawn into the larger struggle for the extension of slavery, the poetic reaction began. The physical and moral pretence of warfare, the cheap splendors of epaulets and feathers, shrivelled at the single touch of the satire of the Biglow Papers. Lowell, writing at that moment with the instinct and fervor of a prophet, brought the whole vainglorious business back to the simple issue of right and wrong:

"'Taint your eppyletts an' feathersMake the thing a grain more right;'Taint afollerin' your bell-wethersWill excuse ye in His sight;Ef you take a sword an' dror it,An' go stick a feller thru,Guv'ment aint to answer for it,God'll send the bill to you."

But far more interesting is the revelation of the American capacity for romance which was made possible by the war between the States. Stevenson's Poems of American History and Stedman's Anthology give abundant illustration of almost every aspect of that epical struggle. The South was in a romantic mood from the very beginning. The North drifted into it after Sumter. I have already said that no one can examine a collection of Civil War verse without being profoundly moved by its evidence of American idealism. In specific phases of the struggle, in connection with certain battle-fields and certain leaders of both North and South, this idealism is heightened into pure romance, so that even our novelists feel that they can give no adequate picture of the war without using the colors of poetry. Most critics, no doubt, agree in feeling that we are still too near to that epoch-making crisis of our national existence to do it any justice in the terms of literature. Perhaps we must wait for the perfected romance of the years 1861-65, until the men and the events of that struggle are as remote as the heroes of Greece and Troy. Certainly no one can pass a final judgment upon the verse occasioned by recent struggles in arms. Any one who has studied the English poetry inspired by the South-African War will be painfully conscious of the emotional and moral complexity of all such issues, of the bitter injustice which poets, as well as other men, render to one another, of the impossibility of transmuting into the pure gold of romance the emotions originating in the stock market, in race-hatred, and in national vainglory.

We have lingered too long, perhaps, over these various evidences of the romantic temper of America. We must now glance at the forces of reaction, the recoil to fact. What is it which contradicts, inhibits, or negatives the romantic tendency? Among other forces, there is certainly humor. Humor and romance often go hand in hand, but humor is commonly fatal to romanticism. There is satire, which rebukes both romanticism and romance, which exposes the fallacies of the one, and punctures the exuberance of the other. More effective, perhaps, than either humor or satire as an antiseptic against romance, is the overmastering sense of fact. This is what Emerson called the instinct for the milk in the pan, an instinct which Emerson himself possessed extraordinarily on his purely Yankee side, and which apioneer country is forced continually to develop and to recognize. Camping, for instance, develops both the romantic sense and the fact sense. Supper must be cooked, even at Walden Pond. There must be hewers of wood and drawers of water, and the dishes ought to be washed.

On a higher plane, also, than this mere sense of physical necessity, there are forces limiting the influence of romance. Schiller put it all into one famous line: —

"Und was uns alle bändigt, das Gemeine."

Or listen to Keats: —

"'T is best to remain aloof from people, and like their good parts, without being eternally troubled with the dull process of their everyday lives.... All I can say is that standing at Charing Cross, and looking East, West, North and South, I can see nothing but dullness."

And Henry James, describing New York in his book, The American Scene, speaks of "the overwhelming preponderance of the unmitigated 'business-man' face ... the consummate monotonous commonness of the pushing male crowd, moving in its dense mass — withthe confusion carried to chaos for any intelligence, any perception; a welter of objects and sounds in which relief, detachment, dignity, meaning, perished utterly and lost all rights ... the universal will to move — to move, move, move, as an end in itself, an appetite at any price."

One need not be a poet like Keats or an inveterate psychologist like Henry James, in order to become aware how the commonplaceness of the world rests like a fog upon the mind and heart. No one goes to his day's work and comes home again without a consciousness of contact with an unspiritual atmosphere, or incompletely spiritualized forces, not merely with indifference, to what Emerson would term "the over-soul," but with a lack of any faith in the things which are unseen. Take those very forces which have limited the influence of Emerson throughout the United States; they illustrate the universal forces which clip the wings of romance. The obstacles in the path of Emerson's influence are not merely the religious and denominational differences which Dr. George A. Gordon portrayed in a notable article at the time of the Emerson Centenary. The real obstacles are more serious. It is true that Dr. Park of Andover, Dr. Bushnell of Hartford, and Dr. Hodge of Princeton, could say in Emerson's lifetime: "We know a better, a more Scriptural and certificated road toward the very things which Emerson is seeking for. We do not grant that we are less idealistic than he. We think him a dangerous guide, following wandering fires. It is better to journey safely with us."

But I have known at least two livery-stable keepers and many college professors who would unite in saying: "Hodge and Park and Bushnell and Emerson are all following after something that does not exist. One is not much more mistaken than the others. We can get along perfectly well in our business without any of those ideas at all. Let us stick to the milk in the pan, the horse in the stall, the documents which you will find in the library."

There exists, in other words, in all classes of American society to-day, just as there existed during the Revolution, during the transcendental movement, or the Civil War, an immense mass of unspiritualized, unvitalized American manhood and womanhood. No literature comes from it and no religion, though there is much human kindness, much material progress, and some indestructible residuum of that idealism which lifts man above the brute.

Yet the curious and the endlessly fascinating thing about these forces of reaction is that they themselves shift and change. We have seen that external romance depending upon strangeness of scene, novelty of adventure, rich atmospheric distance of space or time, disappears with the changes of civilization. The farm expands over the wolf's den, the Indian becomes a blacksmith, but do the gross and material instincts ultimately triumph? He would be a hardy prophet who should venture to assert it. We must reckon always with the swing of the human pendulum, with the reaction against reaction. Here, for example, during the last decade, has been book after book written about the reaction against democracy. All over the world, it is asserted, there are unmistakable signs that democracy will not practically work in the face of the modern tasks to which the world has set itself. One reads these books, one persuades himself that the hour for democracy is passing, and then one goes out on the street and buys a morning newspaper and discovers that democracy has scored again. So is it with the experience of the individual. You may fancy that the romance of the seas passes, for you, with the passing of the square-sailed ship. If Mr. Kipling's poetry cannot rouse you from that mood of reaction, walk down to the end of the pier to-morrow and watch the ocean liner come up the harbor. If there is no romance there, you do not know romance when you see it!

Take the case of the farmer; his prosaic life is the butt of the newspaper paragraphers from one end of the country to the other. But does romance disappear from the farm with machinery and scientific agriculture? There are farmers who follow Luther Burbank's experiments with plants, with all the fascination which used to attach to alchemy and astrology. The farmer has no longer Indians to fight or a wilderness to subdue, but the soils of his farm are analyzed at his state university by men who live in the daily atmosphere of the romance of science, and who say, as a professor in the University of Chicago said once, that "a flower is so wonderful that if you knewwhat was going on within its cell-structure, you would be afraid to stay alone with it in the dark."

The reaction from romance, therefore, real as it is, and dead weight as it lies upon the soul of the nation, often breeds the very forces which destroy it. In other words, the reaction against one type of romance produces inevitably another type of romance, other aspects of wonder, terror, and beauty. Following the romance of adventure comes, after never so deep a trough in the sea, the romance of science, like the crest of another wave; and then comes what we call, for lack of a better word, the psychological romance, the old mystery and strangeness of the human soul, Æschylus and Job, as Victor Hugo says, in the poor crawfish gatherer on the rocks of Brittany.

We must remember that we are endeavoring to measure great spaces and to take account of the "amplitude of time." The individual "fact-man," as Coleridge called him, remains perhaps a fact-man to the end, just as the dreamer may remain a dreamer. But no single generation is compounded all of fact or all of dream. Longfellow felt, no doubt, that there was an ideal United States, which Dickens did not discover during that first visit of 1842; he would have set the Cambridge which he knew over against the

Cincinnati viewed by Mrs. Trollope; he would have asserted that the homes characterized by refinement, by cultivation, by pure and simple sentiment, made up the true America. But even among Longfellow's own contemporaries there was Whitman, who felt that the true America was something very different from that exquisitely tempered ideal of Longfellow. There was Thoreau, who, over in Concord, had been pushing forward the frontier of the mind and senses, who had opened his back-yard gate, as it were, upon the boundless and mysterious territory of Nature. There was Emerson, who was preaching an intellectual independence of the Old World which should correspond to the political and social independence of the Western Hemisphere. There was Parkman, whose hatred of philanthropy, whose lack of spirituality, is a striking illustration of the rebound of New England idealism against itself, of the reaction into stoicism. What different worlds these men lived in, and yet they were all inhabitants, so to speak, of the same parish; most of them met often around the same table! The lesson of their variety of experience and differences of gifts as workmen in that great palace of literature which is so variously built, is that no action and reaction in the imaginative world is ever final. Least of all do these actions and reactions affect the fortunes of true romance. The born dreamer may fall from one dream into another, but he still murmurs, in the famous line of William Ellery Channing, —

"If my bark sinks, 't is to another sea."

No line in our literature is more truly American, — unless it be that other splendid metaphor, by David Wasson, which says the same thing in other words: —

"Life's gift outruns my fancies far,And drowns the dreamIn larger stream,As morning drinks the morning-star."

V
Humor and Satire

A distinguished professor in the Harvard Divinity School once began a lecture on Comedy by saying that the study of the comic had made him realize for the first time that a joke was one of the most solemn things in the world. The analysis of humor is no easy matter. It is hard to say which is the more dreary: an essay on humor illustrated by a series of jokes, or an exposition of humor in the technical terms of philosophy. No subject has been more constantly discussed. But it remains difficult to decide what humor is. It is easier to declare what seemed humorous to our ancestors, or what seems humorous to us to-day. For humor is a shifting thing. The well-known collections of the writings of American humorists surprise us by their revelation of the changes in public taste. Humor—or the sense of humor—alters while we are watching. What seemed a good joke to us yesterday seems but a poor joke to-day. And yet it is the same joke! What is true of the individual is all the more true of the national sense of humor. This vast series of kaleidoscopic changes which we call America; has it produced a humor of its own?

Let us avoid for the moment the treacherous territory of definitions. Let us, rather, take one concrete example: a pair of men, a knight and his squire, who for three hundred years have ridden together down the broad highway of the world's imagination. Everybody sees that Don Quixote and Sancho Panza are humorous. Define them as you will—idealist and realist, knight and commoner, dreamer and proverb-maker—these figures represent to all the world two poles of human experience. A Frenchman once said that all of us are Don Quixotes on one day and Sancho Panzas on the next. Humor springs from this contrast. It is the electric flash between the two poles of experience.

Most philosophers who have meditated upon the nature of the comic point out that it is closely allied with the tragic. Flaubert once compared our human idealism to the flight of a swallow; at one moment it is soaring toward the sunset, at the next moment some one shoots it and it tumbles into the mud with blood upon its glistening wings. The sudden poignant contrast between light, space, freedom, and the wounded bleeding bird in the mud, is of the very essence of tragedy. But something like that is always happening in comedy. There is the same element of incongruity, without the tragic consequence. It is only the humorist who sees things truly because he sees both the greatness and the littleness of mortals; but even he may not know whether to laugh or to cry at what he sees. Those collisions and contrasts out of which the stuff of tragedy is woven, such as the clash between the higher and lower nature of a man, between his past and his present, between one's duties to himself and to his family or the state, between, in a word, his character and his situation, are all illustrated in comedy as completely as in tragedy. The countryman in the city, the city man in the country, is in a comic situation. Here is a coward named Falstaff, and Shakespeare puts him into battle. Here is a vain person, and Malvolio is imprisoned and twitted by a clown. Here is an ignoramus, and Dogberry is placed on the judge's bench. These contrasts might, indeed, be tragic enough, but they are actually comic. Such characters are not ruled by fate but by a sportive chance. The gods connive at them. They are ruled, like tragic characters, by necessity and blindness; but the blindness, instead of leading to tragic ruin, leads only to being caught as in some harmless game of blind-man's-buff. There is retribution, but Falstaff is only pinched by the fairies. Comedy of intrigue and comedy of character lead to no real catastrophe. The end of it on the stage is not death but matrimony; and "home well pleased we go."

A thousand definitions of humor lay stress upon this element of incongruity. Hazlitt begins his illuminating lectures on the Comic Writers by declaring, "Man is the only animal that laughs or weeps; for he is the only animal that is struck with the difference between what things are and what they ought to be." James Russell Lowell took the same ground. "Humor," he said once, "lies in the contrast of two ideas. It is the universal disenchanter. It is the sense of comic contradiction which arises from the perpetual comment which the understanding makes upon the impressions received through the imagination." If that sentence seems too abstract, all we need do is to think of Sancho Panza, the man of understanding, talking about Don Quixote, the man of imagination.

We must not multiply quotations, but it is impossible not to remember the distinction made by Carlyle in writing about Richter. "True humor," says Carlyle, "springs not more from the head than from the heart. It is not contempt; its essence is love." In other words, not merely the great humorists of the world's literature—Cervantes, Rabelais, Fielding, Thackeray, Dickens—but the writers of comic paragraphs for to-morrow's newspaper, all regard our human incongruities with a sort of affection. The comic spirit is essentially a social spirit. The great figures of tragedy are solitary. The immortal figures of comedy belong to a social group.

No recent discussion of humor is more illuminating and more directly applicable to the conditions of American life than that of the contemporary French philosopher Bergson. Bergson insists throughout his brilliant little book on Laughter that laughter is a social function. Life demands elasticity. Hence whatever is stiff, automatic, machine-like, excites a smile. We laugh when a person gives us the impression of being a thing,—a sort of mechanical toy. Every inadaptation of the individual to society is potentially comic. Thus laughter becomes a social initiation. It is a kind of hazing which we visit upon one another. But we do not isolate the comic personage as we do the solitary, tragic figure. The comic personage is usually a type; he is one of an absurd group; he is a miser, a pedant, a pretentious person, a doctor or a lawyer in whom the professional traits have become automatic so that he thinks more of his professional behavior than he does of human health and human justice. Of all these separatist tendencies, laughter is the great corrective. When the individual becomes set in his ways, obstinate, preoccupied, automatic, the rest of us laugh him out of it if we can. Of course all that we are thinking about at the moment is his ridiculousness. But nevertheless, by laughing we become the saviors of society.

No one, I think, can help observing that this conception of humor as incongruity is particularly applicable to a new country. On the new soil and under the new sky, in new social groupings, all the fundamental contrasts and absurdities of our human society assume a new value. We see them under a fresh light. They are differently focussed. The broad humors of the camp, its swift and picturesque play of light and shade, its farce and caricature no less than its atmosphere of comradeship, of sentiment, and of daring, are all transferred to the humor of the newly settled country. The very word "humor" once meant singularity of character, "some extravagant habit, passion, or affection," says Dryden, "particular to some one person." Every newly opened country encourages, for a while, this oddness and incongruity of individual character. It fosters it, and at the same moment it laughs at it. It decides that such characters are "humorous." As the social conditions of such a country change, the old pioneer instinct for humor, and the pioneer forms of humor, may endure, though the actual frontier may have moved far westward.

There is another conception of humor scarcely less famous than the notion of incongruity. It is the conception associated with the name of the English philosopher Hobbes, who thought that humor turned upon a sense of superiority. "The passion of laughter," said Hobbes, "is nothing else but sudden glory arising from some sudden conception of some eminency in ourselves by comparison with the inferiority of others, or with our own formerly." Too cynical a view, declare many critics, but they usually end by admitting that there is a good deal in it after all. I am inclined to think that Hobbes's famous definition is more applicable to wit than it is to humor. Wit is more purely intellectual than humor. It rejoices in its little triumphs. It requires, as has been remarked, a good head, while humor takes a good heart, and fun good spirits. If you take Carlyle literally when he says that humor is love, you cannot wholly share Hobbes's conviction that laughter turns upon a sense of superiority, and yet surely we all experience a sense of kindly amusement which turns upon the fact that we, the initiated, are superior, for the moment, to the unlucky person who is just having his turn in being hazed. It may be the play of intellect or the coarser play of animal spirits. One might venture to make a distinction between the low comedy of the Latin races and the low comedy of the Germanic races by pointing out that the superiority in the Latin comedy usually turns upon quicker wits, whereas the superiority in the Germanic farce is likely to turn upon stouter muscles. But whether it be a play of wits or of actual cudgelling, the element of superiority and inferiority is almost always there.

I remember that some German, I dare say in a forgotten lecture-room, once illustrated the humor of superiority in this way. A company of strolling players sets up its tent in a country village. On the front seat is a peasant, laughing at the antics of the clown. The peasant flatters himself that he sees through those practical jokes on the stage; the clown ought to have seen that he was about to be tripped up, but he was too stupid. But the peasant saw that it was coming all the time. He laughs accordingly. Just behind the peasant sits the village shopkeeper. He has watched stage clowns many a time and he laughs, not at the humor of the farce, but at the naïve laughter of the peasant in front of him. He, the shopkeeper, is superior to such broad and obvious humor as that. Behind the shopkeeper sits the schoolmaster. The schoolmaster is a pedant; he has probably lectured to his boys on the theory of humor, and he smiles in turn at the smile of superiority on the face of the shopkeeper. Well, peeping in at the door of the tent is a man of the world, who glances at the clown, then at the peasant, then at the shopkeeper, then at the schoolmaster, each one of whom is laughing at the others, and the man of the world laughs at them all!

Let us take an even simpler illustration. We all know the comfortable sense of proprietorship which we experience after a few days' sojourn at a summer hotel. We know our place at the table; we call the head waiter by his first name; we are not even afraid of the clerk. Now into this hotel, where we sit throned in conscious superiority, comes a new arrival. He has not yet learned the exits and entrances. He starts for the kitchen door inadvertently when he should be headed for the drawing-room. We smile at him. Why? Precisely because that was what we did on the morning of our own arrival. We have been initiated, and it is now his turn.

If it is true that a newly settled country offers endless opportunities for the humor which turns upon incongruity, it is also true that the new country offers countless occasions for the humor which turns upon the sudden glory of superiority. The backwoodsman is amusing to the man of the settlements, and the backwoodsman, in turn, gets his full share of amusement out of watching the "tenderfoot" in the woods. It is simply the case of the old resident versus the newcomer. The superiority need be in no sense a cruel or taunting superiority, although it often happens to be so. The humor of the pioneers is not very delicately polished. The joke of the frontier tavern or grocery store is not always adapted to a drawing-room audience, but it turns in a surprisingly large number of instances upon exactly the same intellectual or social superiority which gives point to the bon mots of the most cultivated and artificial society in the world.

The humor arising from incongruity, then, and the humor arising from a sense of superiority, are both of them social in their nature. No less social, surely, is the function of satire. It is possible that satire may be decaying, that it is becoming, if it has not already become, a mere splendid or odious tradition. But let us call it a great tradition and, upon the whole, a splendid one. Even when debased to purely party or personal uses, the verse satire of a Dryden retains its magnificent resonance; "the ring," says Saintsbury, "as of a great bronze coin thrown down on marble." The malignant couplets of an Alexander Pope still gleam like malevolent jewels through the dust of two hundred years. The cynicism, the misanthropy, the mere adolescent badness of Byron are powerless to clip the wings of the wide-ranging, far-darting wit and humor and irony of Don Juan. The homely Yankee dialect, the provinciality, the "gnarly" flavor of theBiglow Papers do not prevent our finding in that pungent and resplendent satire the powers of Lowell at full play; and, what is more than that, the epitome of the American spirit in a moral crisis.

Deal Finder

I take the names of those four satirists, Dryden, Pope, Byron, and Lowell, quite at random; but they serve to illustrate a significant principle; namely, that great satire becomes ennobled as it touches communal, not merely individual interests, as it voices social and not merely individual ideals. Those four modern satirists were steeped in the nationalistic political poetry of the Old Testament. They were familiar with its war anthems, dirges, and prophecies, its concern for the prosperity and adversity, the sin and the punishment, of a people. Here the writers of the Golden Age of English satire found their vocabulary and phrase-book, their grammar of politics and history, their models of good and evil kings; and in that Biblical school of political poetry, which has affected our literature from the Reformation down to Mr. Kipling, there has always been a class in satire! The satirical portraits, satirical lyrics, satirical parables of the Old Testament prophets are only less noteworthy than their audacity in striking high and hard. Their foes were the all-powerful: Babylon and Assyria and Egypt loom vast and terrible upon the canvases of Isaiah and Ezekiel; and poets of a later time have learned there the secrets of social and political idealism, and the signs of national doom.

There are two familiar types of satire associated with the names of Horace and Juvenal. Both types are abundantly illustrated in English and American literature. When you meet a bore or a hypocrite or a plain rascal, is it better to chastise him with laughter or to flay him with shining fury? I shall take both horns of the dilemma and assert that both methods are admirable and socially useful. The minor English and American poets of the seventeenth and eighteenth centuries were never weary of speaking of satire as a terrific weapon which they were forced to wield as saviors of society. But whether they belonged to the urbane school of Horace, or to the severely moralistic school of Juvenal, they soon found themselves falling into one or the other of two modes of writing. They addressed either the little audience or the big audience, and they modified their styles accordingly. The great satirists of the Renaissance, for example, like More, Erasmus, and Rabelais, wrote simply for the persons who were qualified to understand them. More and Erasmus wrote their immortal satires in Latin. By so doing they addressed themselves to cultivated Europe. They ran no risk of being misunderstood by persons for whom the joke was not intended. All readers of Latin were like members of one club. Of course membership was restricted to the learned, but had not Horace talked about being content with a few readers, and was not Voltaire coming by and by with the advice to try for the "little public"?

The typical wit of the eighteenth century, whether in London, Paris, or in Franklin's printing-shop in Philadelphia, had, of course, abandoned Latin. But it still addressed itself to the "little public," to the persons who were qualified to understand. The circulation of theSpectator, which represents so perfectly the wit, humor, and satire of the early eighteenth century in England, was only about ten thousand copies. This limited audience smiled at the urbane delicate touches of Mr. Steele and Mr. Addison. They understood the allusions. The fable concerned them and not the outsiders. It was something like Oliver Wendell Holmes reading his witty and satirical couplets to an audience of Harvard alumni. The jokes are in the vernacular, but in a vernacular as spoken in a certain social medium. It is all very delightful.

But there is a very different kind of audience gathering all this while outside the Harvard gates. These two publics for the humorist we may call the invited and the uninvited; the inner circle and the outer circle: first, those who have tickets for the garden party, and who stroll over the lawn, decorously gowned and properly coated, conversing with one another in the accepted social accents and employing the recognized social adjectives; and second, the crowd outside the gates,—curious, satirical, good-natured in the main, straightforward of speech and quick to applaud a ready wit or a humor-loving eye or a telling phrase spoken straight from the heart of the mob.

Will an author choose to address the selected guests or the casual crowd? Either way lies fame, if one does it well. Your uninvited men find themselves talking to the uninvited crowd. Before they know it they are famous too. They are fashioning another manner of speech. Defoe is there, with his saucy ballads selling triumphantly under his very pillory; with his True-Born Englishman puncturing forever the fiction of the honorable ancestry of the English aristocracy; with his Crusoe and Moll Flanders, written, as Lamb said long afterwards, for the servant-maid and the sailor. Swift is there, with his terrific Drapier's Letters, anonymous, aimed at the uneducated, with cold fury bludgeoning a government into obedience; with his Gulliver's Travels, so transparent upon the surface that a child reads the book with delight and remains happily ignorant that it is a satire upon humanity. And then, into the London of Defoe and Swift, and into the very centre of the middle-class mob, steps, in 1724, the bland Benjamin

Franklin in search of a style "smooth, clear, and short," and for half a century, with consummate skill, shapes that style to his audience. His young friend Thomas Paine takes the style and touches it with passion, until he becomes the perfect pamphleteer, and his Crisis is worth as much to our Revolution—men said—as the sword of Washington. After another generation the gaunt Lincoln, speaking that same plain prose of Defoe, Swift, Franklin, and Paine,—Lincoln who began his first Douglas debate, not like his cultivated opponent with the conventional "Ladies and Gentlemen," but with the ominously intimate, "My Fellow Citizens,"—Lincoln is saying, "I am not master of language; I have not a fine education; I am not capable of entering into a disquisition upon dialectics, as I believe you call it; but I do not believe the language I employed bears any such construction as Judge Douglas puts upon it. But I don't care about a quibble in regard to words. I know what I meant, and I will not leave this crowd in doubt, if I can explain it to them, what I really meant in the use of that paragraph."

"I will not leave this crowd in doubt"; that is the final accent of our spoken prose, the prose addressed to one's fellow citizens, to the great public. This is the prose spoken in the humor and satire of Dickens. Dressed in a queer dialect, and put into satirical verse, it is the language of the Biglow Papers. Uttered with the accent of a Chicago Irishman, it is the prose admired by millions of the countrymen of "Mr. Dooley."

Satire written to the "little public" tends toward the social type; that written to the "great public" to the political type. It is obvious that just as a newly settled country offers constant opportunity for the humor of incongruity and the humor arising from a sense of superiority, it likewise affords a daily stimulus to the use of satire. That moralizing Puritan strain of censure which lost none of its harshness in crossing the Atlantic Ocean found full play in the colonial satire of the seventeenth and eighteenth centuries. As the topics for satire grew wider and more political in their scope, the audiences increased. To-day the very oldest issues of the common life of that queer "political animal" named man are discussed by our popular newspaper satirists in the presence of a democratic audience that stretches from the Atlantic to the Pacific.

Is there, then, a distinctly American type of humor and satire? I think it would be difficult to prove that our composite American nationality has developed a mode of humor and satire which is racially different from the humor and satire of the Old World. All racial lines in literature are extremely difficult to draw. If you attempt to analyze English humor, you find that it is mostly Scotch or Irish. If you put Scotch and Irish humor under the microscope, you discover that most of the best Scotch and Irish jokes are as old as the Greeks and the Egyptians. You pick up a copy of Fliegende Blätter and you get keen amusement from its revelation of German humor. But how much of this humor, after all, is either essentially universal in its scope or else a matter of mere stage-setting and machinery? Without the Prussian lieutenant the Fliegende Blätter would lose half its point; nor can one imagine a Punch without a picture of the English policeman. The lieutenant and the policeman, however, are a part of the accepted social furniture of the two countries. They belong to the decorative background of the social drama. They heighten the effectiveness of local humor, but it may be questioned whether they afford any evidence of genuine racial differentiation as to the sense of the comic.

What one can abundantly prove, however, is that the United States afford a new national field for certain types of humor and satire. Our English friends are never weary of writing magazine articles about Yankee humor, in which they explain the peculiarities of the American joke with a dogmatism which has sometimes been thought to prove that there is such a thing as national lack of humor, whether there be such a thing as national humor or not. One such article, I remember, endeavored to prove that the exaggeration often found in American humor was due to the vastness of the American continent. Our geography, that is to say, is too much for the Yankee brain. Mr. Birrell, an expert judge of humor, surely, thinks that the characteristic of American humor lies in its habit of speaking of something hideous in a tone of levity. Many Englishmen, in fact, have been as much impressed with this minimizing trick of American humor as with the converse trick of magnifying. Upon the Continent the characteristic trait of American humor has often been thought to be its exuberance of phrase. Many shrewd judges of our newspaper humor have pointed out that one of its most favorite methods is the suppression of one link in the chain of logical reasoning. Such generalizations as these are always interesting, although they may not take us very far.

Yet it is clear that certain types of humor and satire have proved to be specially adapted to the American soil and climate. Whether or not these types are truly indigenous one may hesitate to say, yet it remains true that the well-known conditions of American life have stimulated certain varieties of humor into such a richness of manifestation as the Old World can scarcely show.

Curiously enough, one of the most perfected types of American humor is that urbane Horatian variety which has often been held to be the exclusive possession of the cultivated and restricted societies of older civilization. Yet it is precisely this kind of humor which has been the delight of some of the most typical American minds. Benjamin Franklin, for example, modelled his style and his sense of the humorous on the papers of the Spectator. He produced humorous fables and apologues, choice little morsels of social and political persiflage, which were perfectly suited, not merely to the taste of London in the so-called golden age of English satire, but to the tone of the wittiest salons of Paris in the age when the old régime went tottering, talking, quoting, jesting to its fall. Read Franklin's charming and wise letter to Madame Brillon about giving too much for the whistle. It is the perfection of well-bred humor: a humor very American, very Franklinian, although its theme and tone and phrasing might well have been envied by Horace or Voltaire.

The gentle humor of Irving is marked by precisely those traits of urbanity and restraint which characterize the parables of Franklin. Does not the Autocrat of the Breakfast Table itself presuppose the existence of a truly cultivated society? Its tone—"As I was saying when I was interrupted"—is the tone of the intimate circle. There was so much genuine humanity in the gay little doctor that persons born outside the circle of Harvard College and the North Shore and Boston felt themselves at once initiated by the touch of his merry wand into a humanized, kindly theory of life. The humor of George William Curtis had a similarly mellow and ripened quality. It is a curious comment upon that theory of Americans which represents us primarily as a loud-voiced, assertive, headstrong people, to be thus made aware that many of the humorists whom we have loved best are precisely those whose writing has been marked by the most delicate restraint, whose theory of life has been the most highly urbane and civilized, whose work is indistinguishable in tone — though its materials are so different — from that of other humorous writers on the other side of the Atlantic. On its social side all this is a fresh proof of the extraordinary adaptability of the American mind. On the literary side it is one more evidence of the national fondness for neatness and perfection of workmanship.

But we are something other than a nation of mere lovers and would-be imitators of Charles Lamb. The moralistic type of humor, the crack of Juvenal's whip, as well as the delicate Horatian playing around the heart-strings, has characterized our humor and satire from the beginning. At bottom the American is serious. Beneath the surface of his jokes there is moral earnestness, there is ethical passion. Take, for example, some of the apothegms of "Josh Billings." He failed with the public until he took up the trick of misspelling his words. When he had once gained his public he sometimes delighted them with sheer whimsical incongruity, like this: —

"There iz 2 things in this life for which we are never fully prepared, and that iz twins."

But more often the tone is really grave. It is only the spelling that is queer. The moralizing might be by La Bruyère or La Rochefoucauld. Take this: —

"Life iz short, but it iz long enuff to ruin enny man who wants tew be ruined."

Or this: —

"When a feller gits a goin doun hill, it dus seem as tho evry thing had bin greased for the okashun." That is what writers of tragedy have been showing, ever since the Greeks!

Or finally, this, which has the perfect tone of the great French moralists: —

"It iz a verry delicate job to forgive a man without lowering him in his own estimashun, and yures too."

See how the moralistic note is struck in the field of political satire. It is 1866, and "Petroleum V. Nasby," writing from "Confedrit X Roads," Kentucky, gives Deekin Pogram's views on education. "He didn't bleeve in edjucashun, generally speekin. The common people was better off without it, ez edjucashun hed a tendency to unsettle their minds. He had seen the evil effex ov it in niggers and poor whites. So soon ez a nigger masters the spellin book and gits into noosepapers, he becomes dissatisfied with his condishin, and hankers after a better cabin and more wages. He towunst begins to insist onto ownin land hisself, and givin his children edjucashun, and, ez a nigger, for our purposes, aint worth a soo markee."

The single phrase, "ez a nigger," spells a whole chapter of American history.

That quotation from "Petroleum V. Nasby" serves also to illustrate a species of American humor which has been of immense historical importance and which has never been more active than it is to-day: the humor, namely, of local, provincial, and sectional types. Much of this falls under Bergson's conception of humor as social censure. It rebukes the extravagance, the rigidity, the unawareness of the individual who fails to adapt himself to his social environment. It takes the place, in our categories of humor, of those types of class humor and satire in which European literature is so rich. The mobility of our population, the constant shifting of professions and callings, has prevented our developing fixed class types of humor. We have not even the lieutenant or the policeman as permanent members of our humorous stock company. The policeman of to-day may be mayor or governor to-morrow. The lieutenant may go back to his grocery wagon or on to his department store. But whenever and wherever such an individual fails to adapt himself to his new companions, fails to take on, as it were, the colors of his new environment, to speak in the new social accents, to follow the recognized patterns of behavior, then the kindly whip of the humorist is already cracking round his ears. The humor and satire of college undergraduate journalism turns mainly upon the recognized ability or inability of different individuals to adapt themselves to their changing pigeon-holes in the college organism. A freshman must behave like a freshman, or he is laughed at. Yet he must not behave as if he were nothing but the automaton of a freshman, or he will be laughed at more merrily still.

One of the first discoveries of our earlier humorists was the Down-East Yankee. "I'm going to Portland whether or no," says Major Jack Downing, telling the story of his boyhood; "I'll see what this world is made of yet. So I tackled up the old horse and packed in a load of ax handles and a few notions, and mother fried me a few doughnuts ... for I told her I didn't know how long I should be gone," — and off he goes to Portland, to see what the world is made of. It is a little like Defoe, and a good deal like the young Ulysses, bent upon knowing cities and men and upon getting the best of bargains.

Each generation of Americans has known something like that trip to Portland. Each generation has had to measure its wits, its resources, its manners, against new standards of comparison. At every stage of the journey there are mishaps and ridiculous adventures; but everywhere, likewise, there is zest, conquest, initiation; the heart of a boy who "wants to know" — as the Yankees used to say; or, in more modern phrase, —

"to admire and for to see,For to behold this world so wide."

There is the same romance of adventure in the humor concerning the Irishman, the Negro, the Dutchman, the Dago, the farmer. Each in turn becomes humorous through failure to adapt himself to the prevalent type. A long-bearded Jew is not ridiculous in Russia, but he rapidly becomes ridiculous even on the East Side of New York. Underneath all this popular humor of the comic supplements one may catch glimpses of the great revolving wheels which are crushing the vast majority of our population into something like uniformity. It is a process of social attrition. The sharp edges of individual behavior get rounded off. The individual loses color and picturesqueness, precisely as he casts aside the national costume of the land from which he came. His speech, his gait, his demeanor, become as nearly as possible like the speech and carriage of all his neighbors. If he resists, he is laughed at; and if he does not personally heed the laughter, he may be sure that his children do. It is the children of our immigrants who catch the sly smiles of their school-fellows, who overhear jokes from the newspapers and on the street corners, who bring home to their foreign-born fathers and mothers the imperious childish demand to make themselves like unto everybody else.

A similar social function is performed by that well-known mode of American humor which ridicules the inhabitants of certain states. Why should New Jersey, for example, be more ridiculous than Delaware? In the eyes of the newspaper paragrapher it unquestionably is, just as Missouri has more humorous connotations than Kentucky. We may think we understand why we smile when a man says that he comes from Kalamazoo or Oshkosh, but the smile when he says "Philadelphia" or "Boston" or "Brooklyn" is only a trifle more subtle. It is none the less real. Why should the suburban dweller of every city be regarded with humorous condescension by the man who is compelled to sleep within the city limits? No one can say, and yet without that humor of the suburbs the comic supplements of American newspapers would be infinitely less entertaining, — to the people who enjoy comic supplements.

So it is with the larger divisions of our national life. Yankee, Southerner, Westerner, Californian, Texan, each type provokes certain connotations of humor when viewed by any of the other types. Each type in turn has its note of provinciality when compared with the norm of the typical American. It is quite possible to maintain that our literature, like our social life, has suffered by this ever-present American sense of the ridiculous. Our social consciousness might be far more various and richly colored, there might be more true provincial independence of speech and custom and imagination if we had not to reckon with this ever-present censure of laughter, this fear of finding ourselves, our city, our section, out of touch with the prevalent tone and temper of the country as a whole. It is one of the forfeits we are bound to pay when we play the great absorbing game of democracy.

We are now ready to ask once more whether there is a truly national type of American humor. Viewed exclusively from the standpoint of racial characteristics, we have seen that this question as to a national type of humor is difficult to answer. But we have seen with equal clearness that the United States has offered a singularly rich field for the development of the sense of humor; and furthermore that there are certain specialized forms of humor which have flourished luxuriantly upon our soil. Our humorists have made the most of their native materials. Every pioneer trait of versatility, curiosity, shrewdness, has been turned somehow to humorous account. The very institutions of democracy, moulding day by day and generation after generation the habits and the mental characteristics of millions of men, have produced a social atmosphere in which humor is one of the most indisputable elements.

I recall a notable essay by Mr. Charles Johnston on the essence of American humor in which he applies to the conditions of American life one familiar distinction between humor and wit. Wit, he asserts, scores off the other man, humor does not. Wit frequently turns upon tribal differences, upon tribal vanity. The mordant wit of the Jew, for example, from the literature of the Old Testament down to the raillery of Heine, has turned largely upon the sense of racial superiority, of intellectual and moral differences. But true humor, Mr. Johnston goes on to argue, has always a binding, a uniting quality. Thus Huckleberry Finn and Jim Hawkins, white man and black man, are afloat together on the Mississippi River raft and they are made brethren by the fraternal quality of Mark Twain's humor. Thus the levelling quality of Bret Harte's humor bridges social and moral chasms. It creates an atmosphere of charity and sympathy. In fact, the typical American humor, according to the opinion of Mr. Johnston, emphasizes the broad and humane side of our common nature. It reveals the common soul.

It possesses a surplusage of power, of buoyancy and of conquest over circumstances. It means at its best a humanizing of our hearts.

Some people will think that all this is too optimistic, but if you are not optimistic enough you cannot keep up with the facts. Certain it is that the pioneers of American national humor, the creators of what we may call the "all-American" type of humor, have possessed precisely the qualities which Mr. Johnston has pointed out. They are apparent in the productions of Artemus Ward. The present generation vaguely remembers Artemus Ward as the man who was willing to send all his wife's relatives to the war and who, standing by the tomb of Shakespeare, thought it "a success." But no one who turns to the almost forgotten pages of that kindly jester can fail to be impressed by his sunny quality, by the atmosphere of fraternal affection which glorifies his queer spelling and his somewhat threadbare witticisms. Mark Twain, who is universally recognized by Europeans as a representative of typical American humor, had precisely those qualities of pioneer curiosity, swift versatility, absolute democracy, which are characteristic of the national temper. His lively accounts of frontier experiences in Roughing It, his comments upon the old world in Innocents Abroad and A Tramp Abroad, his hatred of pretence and injustice, his scorn at sentimentality coupled with his insistence upon the rights of sentiment, in a word his persistent idealism, make Mark Twain one of the most representative of American writers. Largeness, freedom, human sympathy, are revealed upon every page.

It is true that the dangers of American humor are no less in evidence there. There is the danger of extravagance, which in Mark Twain's earlier writings was carried to lengths of absurdity. There is the old danger of the professional humorist of fearing to fail to score his point, and so of underscoring it with painful reiteration. Mark Twain is frequently grotesque. Sometimes there is evidence of imperfect taste, or of bad taste. Sometimes there is actual vulgarity. In his earlier books particularly there is revealed that lack of discipline which has been such a constant accompaniment of American writing. Yet a native of Hannibal, Missouri, trained on a river steamboat and in a country printing-office and in mining-camps, can scarcely be expected to exhibit the finely balanced critical sense of a Matthew Arnold. Mark Twain was often accused in the first years of his international reputation of a characteristically American lack of reverence. He is often irreverent. But here again the boundaries of his irreverence are precisely those which the national instinct itself has drawn. The joke stops short of certain topics which the American mind holds sacred. We all have our favorite pages in the writings of this versatile and richly endowed humorist, but I think no one can read his description of the coyote in Roughing It, and Huckleberry Finn's account of his first visit to the circus, without realizing that in this fresh revelation of immemorial human curiosity, this vivid perception of incongruity and surprise, this series of lightning-like flashes from one pole of experience to the other, we have not only masterpieces of world humor, but a revelation of a distinctly American reaction to the facts presented by universal experience.

The picturesque personality and the extraordinarily successful career of Mark Twain kept him, during the last twenty-five years of his life, in the focus of public attention. But no one can read the pages of the older American humorists,—or try to recall to mind the names of paragraphers who used to write comic matter for this or that newspaper,—without realizing how swiftly the dust of oblivion settles upon all the makers of mere jokes. It is enough, perhaps, that they caused a smile for the moment. Even those humorists who mark epochs in the history of American provincial and political satire, like Seba Smith with his Major Jack Downing, Newell with his Papers of Orpheus C. Kerr, "Petroleum V. Nasby's" Letters from the Confedrit X Roads, Shillaber's Mrs. Partington— all these have disappeared round the turn of the long road.

"Hans Breitman gife a barty—Vhere ish dot barty now?"

It seems as if the conscious humorists, the professional funny writers, had the shortest lease of literary life. They play their little comic parts before a well-disposed but restless audience which is already impatiently waiting for some other "turn." One of them makes a hit with a song or story, just as a draughtsman for a Sunday colored supplement makes a hit with his

"Mutt and Jeff." For a few months everybody smiles and then comes the long oblivion. The more permanent American humor has commonly been written by persons who were almost unconscious, not indeed of the fact that they were creating humorous characters, but unconscious of the effort to provoke a laugh. The smile lasts longer than the laugh. Perhaps that is the secret. One smiles as one reads the delicate sketches of Miss Jewett. One smiles over the stories of Owen Wister and of Thomas Nelson Page. The trouble, possibly, with the enduring qualities of the brilliant humorous stories of "O. Henry" was that they tempt the reader to laugh too much and to smile too little. When one reads the Legend of Sleepy Hollow or Diedrich Knickerbocker's History of New York, it is always with this gentle parting of the lips, this kindly feeling toward the author, his characters and the world. A humorous page which produces that effect for generation after generation, has the stamp of literature. One may doubt whether even the extraordinary fantasies of Mark Twain are more successful, judged by the mere vulgar test of concrete results, than the delicate humor of Charles Lamb. Our current newspaper and magazine humor is in no respect more fascinating than in its suggestion as to the permanent effectiveness of its comic qualities. Who could say, when he first read Mr. Finley P. Dunne's "Mr. Dooley" sketches, whether this was something that a whole nation of readers would instantly and instinctively rejoice over, would find a genial revelation of American characteristics, would recognize as almost the final word of kindly satire upon our overworked, over-excited, over-anxious, over-self-conscious generation?

The range of this contemporary newspaper and magazine humor is well-nigh universal,—always saving, it is true, certain topics or states of mind which the American public cannot regard as topics for laughter. With these few exceptions nothing is too high or too low for it. The paragraphers joke about the wheel-barrow, the hen, the mule, the mother-in-law, the President of the United States. There is no ascending or descending scale of importance. Any of the topics can raise a laugh. If one examines a collection of American parodies, one will find that the happy national talent for fun-making finds full scope in the parody and burlesque of the dearest national sentiments. But no one minds; everybody believes that the sentiments endure while the jokes will pass. The jokes, intended as they are for an immense audience, necessarily lack subtlety. They tend to partake of the methods of pictorial caricature. Indeed, caricature itself, as Bergson has pointed out, emphasizes those "automatic, mechanical-toy" traits of character and behavior which isolate the individual and make him ill adapted for his function in society. Our verbal wit and humor, no less than the pencil of our caricaturists, have this constant note of exaggeration. "These violent delights have violent ends." But during their brief and laughing existence they serve to normalize society. They set up, as it were, a pulpit in the street upon which the comic spirit may mount and preach her useful sermon to all comers.

Despite the universality of the objects of contemporary American humor, despite, too, its prevalent method of caricature, it remains true that its character is, on the whole, clean, easy-going, and kindly. The old satire of hatred has lost its force. No one knows why. "Satirehas grown weak," says Mr. Chesterton, "precisely because belief has grown weak." That is one theory. The late Henry D. Lloyd, of Chicago, declared in one of his last books: "The world has outgrown the dialect and temper of hatred. The style of the imprecatory psalms and the denunciating prophets is out of date. No one knows these times if he is not conscious of this change." That is another theory. Again, party animosities are surely weaker than they were. Caricatures are less personally offensive; if you doubt it, look at any of the collections of caricatures of Napoleon, or of George the Fourth. Irony is less often used by pamphleteers and journalists. It is a delicate rhetorical weapon, and journalists who aim at the great public are increasingly afraid to use it, lest the readers miss the point. In the editorials in the Hearst newspapers, for instance, there is plenty of invective and innuendo, but rarely irony: it might not be understood, and the crowd must not be left in doubt.

Possibly the old-fashioned satire has disappeared because the game is no longer considered worth the candle. To puncture the tire ofpretence is amusing enough; but it is useless to stick tacks under the steam road-roller: the road-roller advances remorselessly and smooths down your mischievous little tacks and you too, indifferently. The huge interests of politics, trade, progress, override your passionate protest. "Shall gravitation cease when you go by?" I do not compare Colonel Roosevelt with gravitation, but have all the satirical squibs against our famous contemporary, from the "Alone in Cubia" to the "Teddy-see," ever cost him, in a dozen years, a dozen votes?

Very likely Mr. Lloyd and Mr. Chesterton are right. We are less censorious than our ancestors were. Americans, on the whole, try to avoid giving pain through speech. The satirists of the golden age loved that cruel exercise of power. Perhaps we take things less seriously than they did; undoubtedly our attention is more distracted and dissipated. At any rate, the American public finds it easier to forgive and forget, than to nurse its wrath to keep it warm. Our characteristic humor of understatement, and our equally characteristic humor of overstatement, are both likely to be cheery at bottom, though the mere wording may be grim enough. No popular saying is more genuinely characteristic of American humor than the familiar "Cheer up. The worst is yet to come."

Whatever else one may say or leave unsaid about American humor, every one realizes that it is a fundamentally necessary reaction from the pressure of our modern living. Perhaps it is a handicap. Perhaps we joke when we should be praying. Perhaps we make fun when we ought to be setting our shoulders to the wheel. But the deeper fact is that most American shoulders are set to the wheel too often and too long, and if they do not stop for the joke they are done for. I have always suspected that Mr. Kipling was thinking of American humor when he wrote in his well-known lines on "The American Spirit": —

"So imperturbable he rulesUnkempt, disreputable, vast — And in the teeth of all the schoolsI — I shall save him at the last."

That is the very secret of the American sense of humor: the conviction that something is going to save us at the last. Otherwise there would be no joke! It is no accident, surely, that the man who is increasingly idolized as the most representative of all Americans, the burden-bearer of his people, the man of sorrows and acquainted with grief, should be our most inveterate humorist. Let Lincoln have his story and his joke, for he had faith in the saving of the nation; and while his Cabinet are waiting impatiently to listen to his Proclamation of Emancipation, give him another five minutes to read aloud to them that new chapter by Artemus Ward.

VI

Individualism and Fellowship

It would be difficult to find a clearer expression of the old doctrine of individualism than is uttered by Carlyle in his London lecture on "The Hero as Man of Letters." Listen to the grim child of Calvinism as he fires his "Annandale grapeshot" into that sophisticated London audience: "Men speak too much about the world.... The world's being saved will not save us; nor the world's being lost destroy us. We should look to ourselves.... For the saving of the world I will trust confidently to the Maker of the world; and look a little to my own saving, which I am more competent to!"

Carlyle was never more soundly Puritanic, never more perfectly within the lines of the moral traditions of his race than in these injunctions to let the world go and to care for the individual soul.

We are familiar with the doctrine on this side of the Atlantic. Here is a single phrase from Emerson's Journal of September, 1833, written on his voyage home from that memorable visit to Europe where he first made Carlyle's acquaintance. "Back again to myself," wrote Emerson, as the five-hundred-ton sailing ship beat her way westward for a long month across the stormy North Atlantic:—"Back again to myself.—A man contains all that is needful to his government within himself. He is made a law unto himself. All real good or evil that can befall him must be from himself.... The purpose of life seems to be to acquaint a man with himself."

In the following August he is writing:—

"Societies, parties, are only incipient stages, tadpole states of men, as caterpillars are social, but the butterfly not. The true and finished man is ever alone."

On March 23, 1835:—

"Alone is wisdom. Alone is happiness. Society nowadays makes us low-spirited, hopeless. Alone is Heaven."

And once more:—

"If Æschylus is that man he is taken for, he has not yet done his office when he has educated the learned of Europe for a thousand years. He is now to approve himself a master of delight to me. If he cannot do that, all his fame shall avail him nothing. I were a fool not to sacrifice a thousand Æschyluses to my intellectual integrity."

These quotations have to do with the personal life. Let me next illustrate the individualism of the eighteen-thirties by the attitude of two famous individualists toward the prosaic question of paying taxes to the State. Carlyle told Emerson that he should pay taxes to the House of Hanover just as long as the House of Hanover had the physical force to collect them, — and not a day longer.

Henry Thoreau was even more recalcitrant. Let me quote him: —

"I have paid no poll-tax for six years. I was put into a jail once on this account, for one night; and, as I stood considering the walls of solid stone, two or three feet thick, the door of wood and iron, a foot thick, and the iron grating which strained the light, I could not help being struck with the foolishness of that institution which treated me as if I were mere flesh and blood and bones, to be locked up. I wondered that it should have concluded at length that this was the best use it could put me to, and had never thought to avail itself of my services in some way. I saw that, if there was a wall of stone between me and my townsmen, there was a still more difficult one to climb or break through before they could get to be as free as I was. I did not for a moment feel confined, and the walls seemed a great waste of stone and mortar. I felt as if I alone of all my townsmen had paid my tax. They plainly did not know how to treat me, but behaved like persons who are underbred. In every threat and in every compliment there was a blunder; for they thought that my chief desire was to stand on the other side of that stone wall. I could not but smile to see how industriously they locked the door on my meditations, which followed them out again without let or hindrance, and they were really all that was dangerous. As they could not reach me, they had resolved to punish my body; just as boys, if they cannot come at some person against whom they have a spite, will abuse his dog. I saw that the State was half-witted, that it was timid as a lone woman with her silver spoons, and that it did not know its friends from its foes, and I lost all my remaining respect for it, and pitied it."

Here is Thoreau's attitude toward the problems of the inner life. The three quotations are from his Walden: —

"Probably I should not consciously and deliberately forsake my particular calling to do the good which society demands of me, to save the universe from annihilation."

"I went to the woods because I wished to live deliberately, to front only the essential facts of life, and see if I could not learn what it had to teach, and not, when I came to die, discover that I had not lived. I did not wish to live what was not life, living is so dear; nor did I wish to practice resignation, unless it was quite necessary. I wanted to live deep and suck out all the marrow of life, to live so sturdily and Spartan-like as to put to rout all that was not life, to cut a broad swath and shave close, to drive life into a corner, and reduce it to its lowest terms, and, if it proved to be mean, why then to get the whole and genuine meanness of it, and publish its meanness to the world; or if it were sublime, to know it by experience, and be able to give a true account of it in my next excursion."

"It is said that the British Empire is very large and respectable, and that the United States are a first-rate power. We do not believe that a tide rises and falls behind every man which can float the British Empire like a chip, if he should ever harbor it in his mind."

All of these quotations from Emerson and Thoreau are but various modes of saying "Let the world go." Everybody knows that in later crises of American history, both Thoreau and Emerson forgot their old preaching of individualism, or at least merged it in the larger doctrine of identification of the individual with the acts and emotions of the community. And nevertheless as men of letters they habitually laid stress upon the rights and duties of the private person. Upon a hundred brilliant pages they preached the gospel that society is in conspiracy against the individual manhood of every one of its members.

They had a right to this doctrine. They came by it honestly through long lines of ancestral heritage. The republicanism of the seventeenth century in the American forests, as well as upon the floor of the English House of Commons, had asserted that private persons had the right to make and unmake kings. The republican theorists of the eighteenth century had insisted that life, liberty, and the pursuit of happiness were the birthright of each individual. This doctrine was related, of course, to the doctrine of equality. If republicanism teaches that "I am as good as others," democracy is forever hinting "Others are as good as I." Democracy has been steadily extending the notion of rights and duties. The first instinct, perhaps, is to ask what is right, just, lawful, for me? Next, what is right, just, lawful for my crowd? That is to say, my family, my clan, my race, my country. The third instinct bids one ask what is right and just and lawful, not merely for me, and for men like me, but for everybody. And when we get that third question properly answered, we can afford to close school-house and church and court-room, for this world's work will have ended.

We have already glanced at various phases of colonial individualism. We have had a glimpse of Cotton Mather prostrate upon the dusty floor of his study, agonizing now for himself and now for the countries of Europe; we have watched Jonathan Edwards in his solitary ecstasies in the Northampton and the Stockbridge woods; we have seen Franklin preaching his gospel of personal thrift and of getting on in the world. Down to the very verge of the Revolution the American pioneer spirit was forever urging the individual to fight for his own hand. Each boy on the old farms had his own chores to do; each head of a family had to plan for himself. The most tragic failure of the individual in those days was the poverty or illness which compelled him to "go on the town." To be one of the town poor indicated that the individualistic battle had been fought and lost. No one ever dreamed, apparently, that a time for old-age pensions and honorable retiring funds was coming. The feeling against any form of community assistance was like the bitter hatred of the workhouse among English laborers of the eighteen-forties.

The stress upon purely personal qualities gave picturesqueness, color, and vigor to the early life of the United States. Take the persons whom Parkman describes in his Oregon Trail. They have the perfect clearness of outline of the portraits by Walter Scott and the great Romantic school of novelists who loved to paint pictures of interesting individual men. There is the same stress upon individualistic portraiture in Irving's Astoria; in the humorous journals of early travellers in the Southern States. It is the secret of the curiosity with which we observe the gamblers and miners and stage-drivers described by Bret Harte. In the rural communities of to-day, in the older portions of the country, and in the remoter settlements of the West and Southwest, the individual man has a sort of picturesque, and, as it were, artistic value, which the life of cities does not allow. The gospel of self-reliance and of solitude is not preached more effectively by the philosophers of Concord than it is by the backwoodsmen, the spies, and the sailors of Fenimore Cooper. Individualism as a doctrine of perfection for the private person and individualism as a literary creed have thus gone hand in hand. "Produce great persons, the rest follows," cried Walt Whitman. He was thinking at the moment about American society and politics. But he believed that the same law held good in poetry. Once get your great man and let him abandon himself to poetry and the great poetry will be the result. It was almost precisely the same teaching as in Carlyle's lecture on "The Hero as Poet."

Well, it is clear enough nowadays that both Whitman and Carlyle underrated the value of discipline. The lack of discipline is the chief obstacle to effective individualism. The private person must be well trained, or he cannot do his work; and as civilization advances, it becomes exceedingly difficult to train the individual without social coöperation. A Paul or a Mahomet may discipline his own soul in the Desert of Arabia; he may there learn the lessons that may later make him a leader of men. But for the average man and indeed for most of the exceptional men, the path to effectiveness lies through social and professional discipline. Here is where the frontier stage of our American life was necessarily weak. We have seen that our ancestors gained something, no doubt, from their spirit of unconventionally and freedom. But they also lost something through their dislike for discipline, their indifference to criticism, their ineradicable tendency, whether in business, in diplomacy, in art and letters and education, to go "across lots." A certain degree of physical orderliness was, indeed, imposed upon our ancestors by the conditions of pioneer life. The natural prodigality and recklessness of frontier existence was here and there sharply checked. Order is essential in a camp, and the thin line of colonies was all camping. A certain instinct for order underlay that resourcefulness which impresses every reader of our history. Did the colonist need a tool? He learned to make it himself. Isolation from the mother country was a stimulus to the inventive imagination. Before long they were maintaining public order in the same ingenious fashion in which they kept house. Appeals to London took too much time. "We send a complaint this year," ran the saying, "the next year they send to inquire, the third year the ministry is changed." No wonder that resourcefulness bred independent action, stimulated the Puritan taste for individualism, and led the way to self-government.

Yet who does not know that the inherent instinct for political order may be accompanied by mental disorderliness? Even your modern Englishman — as the saying goes — "muddles through." The minds of our American forefathers were not always lucid. The mysticism of the New England Calvinists sometimes bred fanaticism. The practical and the theoretical were queerly blended. The essential unorderliness of the American mind is admirably illustrated by that "Father of all the Yankees," Benjamin Franklin. No student of Franklin's life fails to be impressed by its happy casualness, its cheerful flavor of the rogue-romance. Gil Blas himself never drifted into and out of an adventure with a more offhand and imperturbable adroitness. Franklin went through life with the joyous inventiveness of the amateur. He had the amateur's enthusiasm, coupled with a clairvoyant penetration into technical problems such as few amateurs have possessed. With all of his wonderful patience towards other men, Franklin had in the realm of scientific experiment something of the typical impatience of the mere dabbler. He was inclined to lose interest in the special problem before it was worked out. His large, tolerant intelligence was often as unorderly as his papers and accounts. He was a wonderful colonial Jack-of-all-trades; with a range of suggestion, a resourcefulness, a knack of assimilation, a cosmopolitan many-sidedness, which has left us perpetually his debtors. Under different surroundings, and disciplined by a more severe and orderly training, Franklin might easily have developed the very highest order of professional scientific achievement. His natural talent for organization of men and institutions, his "early projecting public spirit," his sense of the lack of formal educational advantages in the colonies, made him the founder of the Philadelphia Academy, the successful agitator for public libraries. Academicism, even in the narrow sense, owes much to this LL.D. of St. Andrews, D.C.L. of Oxford, and intimate associate of French academicians. But one smiles a little, after all, to see the bland printer in this academic company: he deserves his place there, indeed, but he is something more and other than his associates. He is the type of youthful, inexhaustible colonial America; reckless of precedent, self-taught, splendidly alive; worth, to his day and generation, a dozen born academicians; and yet suggesting by his very imperfections, that the Americans of a later day, working under different conditions, are bound to develop a sort of professional skill, of steady, concentrated, ordered intellectual activity, for which Franklin possessed the potential capacity rather than the opportunity and the desire.

Yet there were latent lines of order, hints and prophecies of a coming fellowship, running deep and straight beneath the confused surface of the preoccupied colonial consciousness. In another generation we see the rude Western democracy asserting itself in the valley of the Mississippi. This breed of pioneers, like their fathers on the Atlantic coast line, could turn their hands to anything, because they must. "The average man," says Mr. Herbert Croly, "without any special bent or qualifications, was in the pioneer states the useful man. In that country it was sheer waste to spend much energy upon tasks which demanded skill, prolonged experience, high technical standards, or exclusive devotion.... No special equipment was required. The farmer was obliged to be all kinds of a rough mechanic. The business man was merchant, manufacturer, and storekeeper. Almost everybody was something of a politician. The number of parts which a man of energy played in his time was astonishingly large. Andrew Jackson was successively a lawyer, judge, planter, merchant, general, politician, and statesman; and he played most of these parts with conspicuous success. In such a society a man who persisted in one job, and who applied the most rigorous and exacting standards to his work, was out of place and really inefficient. His finished product did not serve its temporary purpose much better than did the current careless and hasty product, and his higher standards and peculiar ways constituted an implied criticism on the easy methods of his neighbors. He interfered with the rough good-fellowship which naturally arises among a group of men who submit good naturedly and uncritically to current standards. It is no wonder, consequently, that the pioneer Democracy viewed with distrust and aversion the man with a special vocation and high standards of achievement."

The truth of this comment is apparent to everybody. It explains the still lingering popular suspicion of the "academic" type of man. But we are likely to forget that back of all that easy versatility and reckless variety of effort there was some sound and patient and constructive thinking. Lincoln used to describe himself humorously, slightingly, as a "mast-fed" lawyer, one who had picked up in the woods the scattered acorns of legal lore. It was a true enough description, but after all, there were very few college-bred lawyers in the Eighth Illinois Circuit or anywhere else who could hold their own, even in a purely professional struggle, with that long-armed logician from the backwoods.

There was once a "mast-fed" novelist in this country, who scandalously slighted his academic opportunities, went to sea, went into the navy, went to farming, and then went into novel-writing to amuse himself. He cared nothing and knew nothing about conscious literary art; his style is diffuse, his syntax the despair of school-teachers, and many of his characters are bores. But once let him strike the trail of a story, and he follows it like his own Hawkeye; put him on salt water or in the wilderness, and he knows rope and paddle, axe and rifle, sea and forest and sky; and he knows his road home to the right ending of a story by an instinct as sure as an Indian's. Professional novelists like Balzac, professional critics like Sainte-

Beuve, stand amazed at Fenimore Cooper's skill and power. The true engineering and architectural lines are there. They were not painfully plotted beforehand, like George Eliot's. Cooper took, like Scott, "the easiest path across country," just as a bee-hunter seems to take the easiest path through the woods. But the bee-hunter, for all his apparent laziness, never loses sight of the air-drawn line, marked by the homing bee; and your Last of the Mohicans will be instinctively, inevitably right, while your Daniel Deronda will be industriously wrong.

Cooper literally builded better than he knew. Obstinately unacademic in his temper and training, he has won the suffrages of the most fastidious and academic judges of excellence in his profession. The secret is, I suppose, that the lawlessness, the amateurishness, the indifference to standards were on the surface,—apparent to everybody,—the soundness and rightness of his practice were unconscious.

Franklin and Lincoln and Cooper, therefore, may be taken as striking examples of individuals trained in the old happy-go-lucky way, and yet with marked capacities for socialization, for fellowship. They succeeded, even by the vulgar tests of success, in spite of their lack of discipline. But for most men the chief obstacle to effective labor even as individuals is the lack of thoroughgoing training.

It is scarcely necessary to add that there are vast obstacles in the way of individualism as a working theory of society. Carlyle's theory of "Hero Worship" has fewer adherents than for half a century. It is picturesque,— that conception of a great, sincere man and of a world reverencing him and begging to be led by him. But the difficulty is that contemporary democracy does not say to the Hero, as Carlyle thought it must say, "Govern me! I am mad and miserable, and cannot govern myself!"

Democracy says to the Hero, "Thank you very much, but this is our affair. Join us, if you like. We shall be glad of your company. But we are not looking for governors. We propose to govern ourselves."

Even from the point of view of literature and art,—fields of activity where the individual performer has often been felt to be quite independent of his audience,—it is quite evident nowadays that the old theory of individualism breaks down. Even your lyric poet, who more than any other artist stands or sings alone, falls easily into mere lyric eccentricity if he is not bound to his fellows by wholesome and normal ties. In fact, this lyric eccentricity, weakness, wistfulness, is one of the notable defects of American poetry. We have always been lacking in the more objective forms of literary art, like epic and drama. Poe, and the imitators of Poe, have been regarded too often by our people as the normal type of poet. One must not forget the silent solitary ecstasies that have gone into the making of enduring lyric verse, but our literature proves abundantly how soon sweetness may turn to an Emily Dickinson strain of morbidness; how fatally the lovely becomes transformed into the queer. The history of the American short story furnishes many similar examples. The artistic intensity of a Hawthorne, his ethical and moral preoccupations, are all a part of the creed of individualistic art. But both Hawthorne and Poe would have written,—one dare not say better stories, but at least greater and broader and more human stories,—if they had not been forced to walk so constantly in solitary pathways. That fellowship in artistic creation which has characterized some of the greatest periods of art production was something wholly absent from the experience of these gifted and lonely men. Even Emerson and Thoreau wrote "whim" over their portals more often than any artist has the privilege to write it. Emerson never had any thorough training, either in philosophy, theology, or history. He admits it upon a dozen smiling pages. Perhaps it adds to his purely personal charm, just as Montaigne's confession of his intellectual and moral weaknesses heightens our fondness for the Prince of Essayists. But the deeper fact is that not only Emerson and Thoreau, Poe and Hawthorne, but practically every American writer and artist from the beginning has been forced to do his work without the sustaining and heartening touch of national fellowship and pride. Emerson himself felt the chilling poverty in the intellectual and emotional life of the country. He betrays it in this striking passage from his Journal, about the sculptor Greenough:—

"What interest has Greenough to make a good statue? Who cares whether it is good? A few prosperous gentlemen and ladies; but the Universal Yankee

Nation roaring in the capitol to approve or condemn would make his eye and hand and heart go to a new tune."

Those words were written in 1836, but we are still waiting for that new national anthem, sustaining the heart and the voice of the individual artist. Yet there are signs that it is coming.

It is obvious that the day for the old individualism has passed. Whether one looks at art and literature or at the general activities of American society, it is clear that the isolated individual is incompetent to carry on his necessary tasks. This is not saying that we have outgrown the individual. We shall never outgrow the individual. We need for every page of literature and for every adequate performance of society more highly perfected individuals. Some one said of Edgar Allan Poe that he did not know enough to be a great poet. All around us and every day we find individuals who do not know enough for their specific job; men who do not love enough, men in whom the power of will is too feeble. Such men, as individuals, must know and love and will more adequately; and this not merely to perfect their functioning as individuals, but to fulfill their obligations to contemporary society. A true spiritual democracy will never be reached until highly trained individuals are united in the bonds of fraternal feeling. Every individual defect in training, defect in aspiration, defect in passion, becomes ultimately a defect in society.

Let us turn, then, to those conditions of American society which have prepared the way for, and foreshadowed, a more perfect fellowship. We shall instantly perceive the relation of these general social conditions to the specific performances of our men of letters. We have repeatedly noted that our most characteristic literature is what has been called a citizen literature. It is the sort of writing which springs from a sense of the general needs of the community and which has had for its object the safe-guarding or the betterment of the community. Aside from a few masterpieces of lyric poetry, and aside from the short story as represented by such isolated artists as Poe and Hawthorne, our literature as a whole has this civic note. It may be detected in the first writings of the colonists. Captain John Smith's angry order at Jamestown, "He that will not work neither let him eat," is one of the planks in the platform of democracy. Under the trying and depressing conditions of that disastrous settlement at Eden in Martin Chuzzlewit it is the quick wits and the brave heart of Mark Tapley which prove him superior to his employer. The same sermon is preached in Mr. Barrie's play, The Admirable Crichton: cast away upon the desert island, the butler proves himself a better man than his master. This is the motive of a very modern play, but it may be illustrated a hundred times in the history of the seventeenth and eighteenth centuries in America. The practical experiences of the colonists confirmed them in their republican theories. It is true that they held to a doctrine of religious and political individualism. But the moment these theories were put to work in the wilderness a new order of things decreed that this individualism should be modified in the direction of fellowship. Calvinism itself, for all of its insistence upon the value of the individual soul, taught also the principle of the equality of all souls before God. It was thus that the Institutes of Calvin became one of the charters of democracy. The democratic drift in the writings of Franklin and Jefferson is too well known to need any further comment. The triumph of the rebellious colonists of 1776 was a triumph of democratic principles; and although a Tory reaction came promptly, although Hamiltonianism came to stay as a beneficent check to over-radical, populistic theories, the history of the last century and a quarter has abundantly shown the vitality and the endurance of democratic ideas.

One may fairly say that the decade in which American democracy revealed its most ugly and quarrelsome aspect was the decade of the eighteen-thirties. That was the decade when Washington Irving and Fenimore Cooper came home from long sojourns in Europe. They found themselves confronted at once by sensitive, suspicious neighbors who hated England and Europe and had a lurking or open hostility towards anything that savored of Old World culture. Yet in that very epoch when English visitors were passing their most harsh and censorious verdict upon American culture, Emerson was writing in his Journal (June 18, 1834) a singular prophecy to the effect that the evils of our democracy, so far as literature was concerned, were to be cured by the remedy of more democracy. Is it not striking that he turns away from the universities and the traditional culture of New England and looks towards the Jacksonism of the new West to create a new and native American literature? Here is the passage:—

"We all lean on England; scarce a verse, a page, a newspaper, but is writ in imitation of English forms; our very manners and conversation are traditional, and sometimes the life seems dying out of all literature, and this enormous paper currency of Words is accepted instead. I suppose the evil may be cured by this rank rabble party, the Jacksonism of the country, heedless of English and of all literature—a stone cut out of the ground without hands;—they may root out the hollow dilettantism of our cultivation in the coarsest way, and the new-born may begin again to frame their own world with greater advantage."

From that raw epoch of the eighteen-thirties on to the Civil War, one may constantly detect in American writing the accents of democratic radicalism. Partly, no doubt, it was a heritage of the sentiment of the French Revolution. "My father," said John Greenleaf Whittier, "really believed in the Preamble of the Bill of Rights, which re-affirmed the Declaration of Independence." So did the son! Equally clear in the writings of those thirty years are echoes of the English radicalism which had so much in common with the democratic movement across the English Channel. The part which English thinkers and English agitators played in securing for America the fruits of her own democratic principles has never been adequately acknowledged.

That the outcome of the Civil War meant a triumph of democratic ideas as against aristocratic privilege, no one can doubt. There were no stancher adherents of the democratic idea than our intellectual aristocrats. The best Union editorials at the time of the Civil War, says James Ford Rhodes, were written by scholars like Charles Eliot Norton and James Russell Lowell. I think it was Lowell who once said, in combatting the old aristocratic notion of white man supremacy, that no gentleman is willing to accept privileges that are inaccessibleto other men. This is precisely like the famous sentence of Walt Whitman which first arrested the attention of "Golden Rule Jones," the mayor of Toledo, and which made him not only a Whitmaniac for the rest of his life but one of the most useful of American citizens. The line was,

"I will accept nothing which all may not have their counterpart of on the same terms."

This instinct of fellowship cannot be separated, of course, from the older instincts of righteousness and justice. It involves, however, more than giving the other man his due. It means feeling towards him as towards another "fellow." It involves the sentiment of partnership. Historians of early mining life in California have noted the new phase of social feeling in the mining-camps which followed upon the change from the pan—held and shaken by the solitary miner—to the cradle, which required the coöperation of at least two men. It was when the cradle came in that the miners first began to say "partner." As the cradle gave way to placer mining, larger and larger schemes of coöperation came into use. In fact, Professor Royce has pointed out in his History of California that the whole lesson of California history is precisely the lesson most necessary to be learned by the country as a whole, namely, that the phase of individual gain-getting and individualistic power always leads to anarchy and reaction, and that it becomes necessary, even in the interests of effective individualism itself, to recognize the compelling and ultimate authority of society.

What went on in California between 1849 and 1852 is precisely typical of what is going on everywhere to-day. American men and women are learning, as we say, "to get together." It is the distinctly twentieth-century programme. We must all learn the art of getting together, not merely to conserve the interests of literature and art and society, but to preserve the individual himself in his just rights. Any one who misunderstands the depth and the scope of the present political restlessness which is manifested in every section of the country, misunderstands the American instinct for fellowship. It is a law of that fellowship that what is right and legitimate for me is right and legitimate for the other fellow also. The American mind and the American conscience are becoming socialized before our very eyes. American art and literature must keep pace with this socialization of the intelligence and the conscience, or they will be no longer representative of the true America.

Literary illustrations of this spirit of fraternalism lie close at hand. They are to be found here and there even in the rebellious, well-nigh anarchic, individualism of the Concord men. They are to be found throughout the prose and verse of Whittier. No one has preached a truer or more effective gospel of fellowship than Longfellow, whose poetry has been one of the pervasive influences in American democracy, although Longfellow had but little to say about politics and never posed in a slouch hat and with his trousers tucked into his boots. Fellowship is taught in the Biglow Papers of Lowell and the stories of Mrs. Stowe. It is wholly absent from the prose and verse of Poe, and it imparts but a feeble warmth to the delicately written pages of Hawthorne. But in the books written for the great common audience of American men and women, like the novels of Winston Churchill; and in the plays which have scored the greatest popular successes, like those of Denman Thompson, Bronson Howard, Gillette, Augustus Thomas, the doctrine of fellowship is everywhere to be traced. It is in the poems of James Whitcomb Riley and of Sam Walter Foss; in the work of hundreds of lesser known writers of verse and prose who have echoed Foss's sentiment about living in a "house by the side of the road" and being a "friend of man."

To many readers the supreme literary example of the gospel of American fellowship is to be found in Walt Whitman. One will look long before one finds a more consistent or a nobler doctrine of fellowship than is chanted in Leaves of Grass. It is based upon individualism; the strong body and the possessed soul, sure of itself amid the whirling of the "quicksand years"; but it sets these strong persons upon the "open road" in comradeship; it is the sentiment of comradeship which creates the indissoluble union of "these States"; and the States, in turn, in spite of every "alarmist," "partialist," or "infidel," are to stretch out unsuspicious and friendly hands of fellowship to the whole world. Anybody has the right to call Leaves of Grass poor poetry, if he pleases; but nobody has the right to deny its magnificent Americanism.

It is not merely in literature that this message of fellowship is brought to our generation. Let me quote a few sentences from the recent address of

George Gray Barnard, the sculptor, in explaining the meaning of his marble groups now placed at the entrance to the Capitol of Pennsylvania. "I resolved," says Barnard, "that I would build such groups as should stand at the entrance to the People's temple ... the home of those visions of the ever-widening and broadening brotherhood that gives to life its dignity and its meaning. Life is told in terms of labor. It is fitting that labor, its triumphs, its message, should be told to those who gaze upon a temple of the people. The worker is the hope of all the future. The needs of the worker, his problems, his hopes, his untold longings, his sacrifices, his triumphs, all of these are the field of the art of the future. Slowly we are groping our way towards the new brotherhood, and when that day dawns, men will enter a world made a paradise by labor. Labor makes us kin. It is for this reason that there has been placed at the entrance of this great building the message of the Adam and Eve of the future, the message of labor and of fraternity."

That there are defects in this gospel and programme of American fellowship, every one is aware. If the obstacle to effective individualism is lack of discipline, the obstacles to effective fellowship are vagueness, crankiness, inefficiency, and the relics of primal selfishness. Nobody in our day has preached the tidings of universal fellowship more fervidly and powerfully than Tolstoï. Yet when one asks the great Russian, "What am I to do as a member of this fellowship?" Tolstoï gives but a confused and impractical answer. He applies to the complex and contradictory facts of our contemporary civilization the highest test and standard known to him: namely, the principles of the New Testament. But if you ask him precisely how these principles are to be made the working programme of to-morrow, the Russian mysticism and fanaticism settle over him like a fog. We pass Tolstoïans on the streets of our American cities every day; they have the eyes of dreamers, of those who would build, if they could, a new Heaven and a new Earth. But they do not know exactly how to go about it. Our practical Western minds seize upon some actual plan for constructive labor. Miss Jane Addams organizes her settlements in the slums; Booker Washington gives his race models of industrial education; President Eliot has a theory of university reform and then struggles successfully for forty years to put that theory into practice. Compared with the concrete performance of such social workers as these, the gospel according to Whitman and Tolstoï is bound to seem vague in its outlines, and ineffective in its concrete results. That such a gospel attracts cranks and eccentrics of all sorts is not to be wondered at. They come and go, but the deeper conceptions of fraternalism remain.

A further obstacle to the progress of fellowship lies in selfishness. But let us see how even the coarser and rawer and cruder traits of the American character may be related to the spirit of common endeavor which is slowly transforming our society, and modifying, before our eyes, our contemporary art and literature.

"The West," says James Bryce, "is the most American part of America, that is to say the part where those features which distinguish America from Europe come out in the strongest relief." We have already noted in our study of American romance how the call of the West represented for a while the escape from reality. The individual, following that retreating horizon which we name the West, found an escape from convention and from social law. Beyond the Mississippi or beyond the Rockies meant to him that "somewheres east of Suez" where the Ten Commandments are no longer to be found, where the individual has free rein. But by and by comes the inevitable reaction, the return to reality. The pioneer sobers down; he finds that "the Ten Commandments will not budge"; he sees the need of law and order; he organizes a vigilance committee; he impanels a jury, even though the old Spanish law does not recognize a jury. The new land settles to its rest. The output of the gold mines shrinks into insignificance when compared with the cash value of crops of hay and potatoes. The old picturesque individualism yields to a new social order, to the conception of the rights of the state. The story of the West is thus an epitome of the individual human life as well as the history of the United States.

We have been living through a period where the mind of the West has seemed to be the typical national mind. We have been indifferent to traditions. We have overlooked the defective training of the individual, provided he "made good." We have often, as in the free silver craze, turned our back upon universal experience. We have been recklessly deaf to the teachings of history; we have spoken of the laws of literature and art as if they were mere conventions designed to oppress the free activity of the artist. Typical utterances of our writers are Jack London's "I want to get away from the musty grip of the past," and Frank Norris's "I do not want to write literature, I want to write life."

The soul of the West, and a good deal of the soul of America, has been betrayed in words like those. Not to share this hopefulness of the West, its stress upon feeling rather than thinking, its superb confidence, is to be ignorant of the constructive forces of the nation. The humor of the West, its democracy, its rough kindness, its faith in the people, its generous notion of "the square deal for everybody," its elevation of the man above the dollar, are all typical of the American way of looking at the world. Typical also, is its social solidarity, its swift emotionalism of the masses. It is the Western interest in the ethical aspect of social movements that is creating some of the moving forces in American society to-day. Experiment stations of all kinds flourish on that soil. Chicago newspapers are more alive to new ideas than the newspapers of New York or Boston. No one can understand the present-day America if he does not understand the men and women who live between the Allegheny Mountains and the Rocky Mountains. They have worked out, more successfully than the composite population of the East, a general theory of the relation of the individual to society; in other words, a combination of individualism with fellowship.

To draw up an indictment against this typical section of our country is to draw up an indictment against our people as a whole. And yet one who studies the literature and art produced in the great Mississippi Valley will see, I believe, that the needs of the West are the real needs of America. Take that commonness of mind and tone, which friendly foreign critics, from De Tocqueville to Bryce, have indicated as one of the dangers of our democracy. This commonness of mind and tone is often one of the penalties of fellowship. It may mean a levelling down instead of a levelling up.

Take the tyranny of the majority,—to which Mr. Bryce has devoted one of his most suggestive chapters. You begin by recognizing the rights of the majority. You end by believing that the majority must be right. You cease to struggle against it. In other words, you yield to what Mr. Bryce calls "the fatalism of the multitude." The individual has a sense of insignificance. It is vain to oppose the general current. It is easier to acquiesce and to submit. The sense of personal responsibility lessens. What is the use of battling for one's own opinions when one can already see that the multitude is on the other side? The greater your democratic faith in the ultimate rightness of the multitude, the less perhaps your individual power of will. The easier is it for you to believe that everything is coming out right, whether you put your shoulder to the wheel or not.

The problem of overcoming these evils is nothing less than the problem of spiritualizing democracy. There are some of our hero-worshipping people who think that that vast result can still be accomplished by harking back to some such programme as the "great man" theory of Carlyle. Another theory of spiritualizing democracy, no less familiar to the student of nineteen-century literature, is what is called "the divine average" doctrine of Walt Whitman. The average man is to be taught the glory of his walk and trade. Round every head there is to be an aureole. "A common wave of thought and joy, lifting mankind again," is to make us forget the old distinction between the individual and the social group. We are all to be the sons of the morning.

We must not pause to analyze or to illustrate these two theories. Carlyle's theory seems to me to be outworn, and Whitman's theory is premature. But it is clear that they both admit that the mass of men are as yet incompletely spiritualized, not yet raised to their full stature. Unquestionably, our American life is, in European eyes at least, monotonously uniform. It is touched with self-complacency. It is too intent upon material progress. It confuses bigness with greatness. It is unrestful. It is marked by intellectual impatience. Our authors are eager to write life rather than literature. But they are so eager that they overlook the need of literary discipline. They do not learn to write literature and therefore most of them are incapable of interpreting life. They escape, perhaps, from "the musty grip of the past," but in so doing they refuse to learn the inexorable lessons of the past. Hence the fact that our books lack power, that they are not commensurate with the living forces of the country.

The unconscious, moral, and spiritual life of the nation is not back of them, making "eye and hand and heart go to a new tune."

If we could have that, we should ask no more, for we believe in the nation. I heard a doctor say, the other day, that a man's chief lesson was to pull his brain down into his spinal cord; that is to say, to make his activities not so much the result of conscious thought and volition, as of unconscious, reflex action; to stop thinking and willing, and simply do what one has to do. May there not be a hint here of the ultimate relation of the individual to the social organism; the relation of our literature to our national character?

There is a period, no doubt, when the individual must painfully question himself, test his powers, and acquire the sense of his own place in the world. But there also comes a more mature period when he takes that place unconsciously, does his work almost without thinking about it, as if it were not his work at all.

The brain has gone down into the spinal cord; the man is functioning as apart of the organism of society; he has ceased to question, to plan, to decide; it is instinct that does his work for him.

Literature and art, at their noblest, function in that instinctive way. They become the unconscious expression of a civilization. A nation passes out of its adolescent preoccupation with plans and with materials.

It learns to do its work, precisely as Goethe bade the artist do his task, without talking about it. We, too, shall outgrow in time our questioning, our self-analysis, our futile comparison of ourselves with other nations, our self-conscious study of our own national character.

We shall not forget the distinction between "each" and "all," but "all" will increasingly be placed at the service of "each." With fellowship based upon individualism, and with individualism ever leading to fellowship, America will perform its vital tasks, and its literature will be the unconscious and beautiful utterance of its inner life.

9 781835 915608